WEST POINT TO WALL STREET

WEST POINT —TO— WALL STREET

My Journey To Mental Wellness

OMAR RITTER

COPYRIGHT © 2025 OMAR RITTER

All rights reserved. No part of this book may be used or reproduced in any form whatsoever without written permission except in the case of brief quotations in critical articles or reviews.

To book a speaking event, contact:
www.omarritter.com

WEST POINT TO WALL STREET
My Journey to Mental Wellness

FIRST EDITION

ISBN 978-1-5445-4867-8 *Hardcover*
      978-1-5445-4866-1 *Paperback*
      978-1-5445-4868-5 *Ebook*

Cover design by Michael Nagin

This book is dedicated to all those lost to war or mental health struggles, whether military or civilian. Your sacrifices and battles, seen and unseen, will never be forgotten.

I also dedicate this book to my dear friend and West Point classmate Gary Williams, whose life was tragically cut short in a motor-vehicle accident on May 5, 2025. Gary, your unwavering spirit and friendship continue to inspire me, and your memory will forever live on in our hearts.

May this book serve as a beacon of hope and resilience for those navigating their own journeys. You are not alone.

CONTENTS

INTRODUCTION 9

PART I: LAYING THE FOUNDATION
1. THE BROKEN PATH 13
2. EXTRA! EXTRA! 33
3. AN UPHILL CLIMB 47

PART II: MAKING OF A SOLDIER
4. WEST POINT 67
5. FORWARD, MARCH! 85
6. THE POWER OF RELATIONSHIPS 95
7. NEXT STOP, KOSOVO 111
8. FROM PEACEKEEPING TO COMBAT 123
9. UNDER FIRE 135

PART III: BATTLING ON THE HOME FRONT
10. HOW DID I GET HERE? 157
11. DETOUR AHEAD 181
12. THE PATH FROM HERE 199

CONTACT ME 215
ADDITIONAL RESOURCES 217
ABOUT THE AUTHOR 219

INTRODUCTION

IN A WORLD WHERE RESILIENCE IS TESTED OFTEN AND personal struggles can feel insurmountable, the journey toward healing and growth can become a profound quest woven throughout the fabric of our entire lives. This book is a testament to that journey—a journey that belongs not just to me but to everyone who has faced adversity and emerged, though perhaps battered, with a newfound strength and purpose.

I invite you to walk alongside me as I share my story, one that began in humble surroundings and unfolded through a less-than-stable childhood, military service, brain surgery, the intensity of the Columbia MBA program, Wall Street, and debilitating battles with my mental health. Each chapter reflects not just my personal experiences but universal truths about resilience, courage, and the transformative power of vulnerability.

My journey has been shaped by the adversities I've faced, including an over-twenty-year struggle with post-traumatic stress disorder (PTSD), which ignited within me a passion to break the stigma surrounding mental healthcare. As I delve into the lessons I've learned on the winding road of my life, I hope to empower you to confront your own challenges and embrace a journey of self-discovery and healing.

Together, let's explore the wisdom born from life's toughest moments. Let the pages of this book be a source of inspiration, a reminder you are not alone, and a guide to lead you toward resilience and personal growth. Welcome to a narrative that champions hope, courage, and the unwavering human spirit while acknowledging we each may need some help navigating this journey called life.

Part I

LAYING THE FOUNDATION

CHAPTER 1

THE BROKEN PATH

WE ALL HAVE A STORY TO TELL. SOME OF US ARE BRAVE ENOUGH to share ours with the world, standing tall as we recount our experiences and lessons learned. But this bravery often comes with subtle deceptions. We find ourselves tweaking our stories to suit our audience, changing details to elicit a desired response, entertain, or fit in. With each retelling, these alterations can blur the truth, and the real story is lost somewhere along the way.

Others decide not to talk about their pasts. They bury their stories deep within, sealing them in a graveyard of memories they rarely visit. They may do this to protect themselves from painful memories or because they believe their pasts are irrelevant to their presents. Silence becomes a shield, a way to maintain control over what is shared and what is hidden.

I belong to a third category. I embrace my story wholeheartedly—even the parts that scarred me—deriving strength and motivation from the experiences that shaped me. My journey, with all its ups and downs, has taught me resilience, empathy, and courage. As I sit down to recall my steps down this road so far, I find emotions and lessons that have played a profound role in my transformation right from the very beginning.

NAVIGATING CHILDHOOD CHALLENGES

In the beginning—I strongly advocate for keeping families TOGETHER

Reflecting on the past that shaped my life, each memory brings a wave of emotions. I find the most vivid and impactful memories, though, are the ones from my childhood. Many have written about the significance of this phase, filled with wonder and discovery, as the most formative period of a person's life. It shapes who we become and which paths we take or avoid in the future. For me, the amazement and joy of childhood were often obscured by the adjustments and compromises that come with constantly moving.

I think this happens to all children whose parents decide to separate when the child is still very young. I was just five years old when my parents divorced. I was a boy who dreamt of becoming the most remarkable man to walk the earth, who constantly thought of himself as a superhero or the next great athlete. In other words: a normal five-year-old. At such a tender age, a child's world is usually filled with hopes and dreams, the most important being that their parents show love and unity. The breakup of my family was a shocking experience, one that left a significant mark on my young heart and my ambitious dreams.

Even today, I can vividly remember the confusion and sadness that filled my life during that period. The expectation that my parents would always be together, the plans and dreams we had for our shared future, the laughter around the dinner table, and the stories that played an essential role in making my childhood awesome were replaced by constant complaints, hushed conversations, closed doors, yelling, and a lot of crying.

The atmosphere was tense, and I could sense something was wrong, even if I didn't fully comprehend what. I longed for the days when we would all sit together around the table eating dinner while my father and mother talked about work or what they had planned for the weekend—the mundanity that creates the warmth of a home. I wanted that predictability back, the calm that had been replaced by chaos.

WHEN LOVE ISN'T ENOUGH

Elementary school in Germany: the calm before the storm. I'm front row on the left.

It cannot be said that my parents never loved each other. They met during college, young and full of dreams. Their shared goals and sense of adventure attracted them to each other, and their love snowballed. My dad was handsome and outgoing, and my mother was an attractive, smart, and petite woman who knew how to carry herself well. It wasn't long before they married and started a life together. The love and attraction they shared inspired the years they spent together and the family they grew to include three children.

Shortly after being married, my father's work with the army took them to Germany, where my brothers and I were born. Those early years in Germany were both challenging and rewarding for my parents. My father's military career provided a stable foundation for our family. At the same time, my mother worked as a government accountant, a profession she was passionate about as it stimulated her mind and allowed her to retreat from domestic life a few hours a day. Those were the good old days. Life was simple, following a routine that offered a sense of security and order.

The initial days in Germany were fun. During the Cold War, the US military bases across Europe had numerous parks and activities for kids. In the beginning, my family was happy to experience Germany. We felt fortunate to be exposed to a new culture and way of life. My mother often spoke fondly of the charming villages, lively markets, and rich history that surrounded us. On weekends, she would take my brothers—Ronald, my older brother, and Khatib, my younger brother—and me on walks through the beautiful streets and markets. Grocery shopping at German stores was always a fun event for Mom and us kids; life was good.

However, my brothers and I didn't realize that beneath the surface of our idyllic life, underlying tensions were slowly unraveling the fabric of my parents' marriage. My father, with his military background, was a man of extreme discipline. His approach to life was regimented and precise, with every detail meticulously planned and executed. At times, this approach turned into rigid demands and almost impossibly high standards. For him, perfection meant everything, and so did order.

My father's obsessive-compulsive tendencies and desire for obedience often clashed with the unpredictability and messiness of family life. He had routines that had to be followed precisely, and any deviation from these routines could trigger frustration and tension. While my mother admired his dedication and focus, she found it increasingly difficult to live under the weight of his expectations. He transformed into a relentless drill sergeant, demanding discipline around the clock, every day of the week. With each passing day, his control over our lives frustrated my mother more and more. I could see it in her face; she was tired. Then, they stopped talking to each other, and I noticed Dad often slept on the couch or stayed overnight at work. These were the early signs of their marriage falling apart.

The pressure of maintaining a perfectly ordered life took its toll on my mother. She was a woman of great patience and resilience, but the constant need to adhere to my father's strict standards wore on her. She grappled with finding equilibrium between supporting his wants and needs and preserving her own identity. Although her work offered a bit of an escape, a space where she could express her independence and capabilities, the challenges at home often overshadowed her professional achievements.

As time went on, the strain on their marriage became more visible. My parents struggled to establish common ground for communication. I noticed my mother tiptoeing to avoid disagreements, while my father busied himself with extra work and socializing, often staying away from home. My father's frequent absence placed all the responsibilities of raising three young boys solely on my mother's shoulders much of the time. Although my parents deeply loved each other, their incompatible personalities and perspectives gradually caused a rift to form between them, and time only widened it.

Ultimately, my mother chose to end the marriage, prioritizing her peace of mind and personal growth over maintaining an unhealthy relationship. The decision to depart was a challenging one, but leaving was essential for her to reclaim her individuality and pursue a path toward self-realization. She put her own well-being first—something many struggle to do as they navigate life's challenges.

TORN BETWEEN WORLDS

My parents had to decide whether my brothers and I would move with my mother to South Carolina or stay with my father in Germany. These types of decisions are heart-wrenching for a child, especially when there is significant physical distance between the parents. Personally, it forced me to confront the painful reality that my parents' bond, the bond that had built our family, the bond I had taken for granted would always be there, no longer existed. I felt torn between two worlds, each filled with love and yet so different from what I had known.

I was told my brothers and I would leave with my mother. The rationale was that my father was constantly on the move with his military career, and my brothers and I would be better off in South Carolina, where my mother had family who could help care for us. For me, it didn't matter which option they chose. I was separated from one parent no matter where I lived. So, I went along with the plan and supported my mother as best I could during our relocation to South Carolina.

My heart broke over and over again as my mother packed our bags, every moment feeling like a slow-motion tragedy. As we prepared to depart, the immense weight of leaving my hero, my dad, thousands of miles away sank deep. But this phase of my life taught me a great lesson: Love, while powerful, is not always enough to overcome deeply ingrained incompatibilities. Sometimes, all the love and good wishes in the world are insufficient to repair a damaged relationship, no matter how fervently one may wish otherwise.

WORLDS APART

From the time we moved to South Carolina when I was five, until fifth grade, I lived with my mother, two brothers, and two maternal great-grandparents. Our modest three-bedroom, one-bathroom house was filled with the bustling activity and warmth of family life, hosting up to fifty family members each Thanksgiving. The house itself held sentimental value for my family as my great-grandmother received the down payment from a Caucasian family she worked for as a nanny for over two decades in Georgia. I have since paid off the house and now own it. Despite the confined space, where my brothers, mother, and I shared a single bedroom, it provided a sense of comfort and security in our new environment.

The beginning days in South Carolina were very awkward for me. I felt like a fish out of water, trying to find my place in a setting so different from what I had known and grown up in. I missed the familiarity of Germany—the comforting routines, familiar faces, and sense of belonging that had been such constant parts of my life there. The transition from Germany to South Carolina was a significant change, and I longed for the life we had left behind.

One of the things I missed most was time spent with my father. This was a tough adjustment for a boy who had previously enjoyed daily access to his dad and wanted to do "guy" things. Our life in Germany was a mixture of discipline and warmth, with my father playing a central role in our family. Despite his strict nature, he had a unique way of making ordinary days feel like grand adventures.

I fondly remember weekends when he would take us on excursions or listen to old jazz and soul albums. He could play the piano, trumpet, and saxophone and even sing. Unfortunately, I inherited none of these talents.

My dad told me stories from his childhood filled with dreams and aspirations that sparked my imagination and made me believe anything was possible. This sense of hope has never left me as I believe the United States of America is a place where dreams can come true if you pursue them passionately.

I felt no one could replace my father in my life, especially at the beginning of the transition. His absence left a void that was difficult to fill. I missed his reassuring presence, his tapping me on the shoulder to prove a point, and the way he lit up a room when he was happy. I longed for when he would sit with me and my brothers and share his dreams for the future—plans for grand houses, sleek cars, and a life filled with possibilities. Even though many of those dreams never came to fruition, the hope and excitement he instilled in us were irreplaceable.

In those early days, I often felt as if I were living in two worlds: the world of my memories of Germany and the reality of our new life in South Carolina. The landscape around me was unfamiliar. Germany's rolling hills, mountain ranges, and dense forests had been replaced by pine forests and wetlands sprawled over the flat, low-lying terrain of Summerville, South Carolina. The weather was also completely different from what I had grown accustomed to in Germany. The humid, subtropical climate felt like a far cry from the temperate seasons I had known, with long, hot summers that left me yearning for the cooler days of my past.

Although South Carolina is beautiful, with its lush greenery and summer atmosphere, it took some time for me to adjust to this new life. The small town we moved to was charming, but it lacked the vibrant energy of the cities I had known in Germany. Additionally, South Carolina in the 1980s was not very diverse, primarily consisting of African American and Caucasian residents, compared to the multicultural environment of the military. The sounds of cicadas and scent of magnolia blossoms were also new to me, adding another layer of unfamiliarity to my surroundings.

EMBRACING SOUTH CAROLINA

Time heals everything, or so they say. In just a few weeks, I began to adapt to my new life in South Carolina. The initial awkwardness and homesickness faded as I established a new routine, and the unfamiliarity of my surroundings gradually transformed into a sense of home. As the days turned into weeks, I found my rhythm in this Southern state.

School became a significant part of my life, a place to grow academically and socially. Initially, finding my place was a challenge, but I slowly started making friends. I'm proud to say I was one of the few kids with a diverse friend group, focusing on people rather than skin color when socializing. I was eager to share stories about my life in Germany, and many kids were curious about my experiences and captivated by my descriptions of the culture I had come from, which helped me connect with my new peers and smooth my transition.

The Summerville community during this period was known for its warmth and hospitality, but the reality was much more nuanced. Some of the people I cherished most bore no resemblance to me. The street I lived on, which is now very gentrified, was in the African American section of town in the 1980s and 1990s. The neighborhood exuded true Southern hospitality; everyone knew each other, and doors were often left unlocked.

Community events typically included Sunday school for the kids followed by church services and a Sunday dinner at 1:00 p.m. My great-grandfather and great-grandmother were highly regarded as a deacon and deaconess at the church. Neighborhood gatherings were usually a welcoming setting. To truly connect with our neighbors, we embraced these customs and traditions, gradually becoming an integral part of this vibrant community. Even at a young age, I yearned for a more diverse environment, but for now, I had to work with the community I had.

ROOTS IN ADAMS RUN, SOUTH CAROLINA

My connection to the area deepened through my family, particularly my grandfather, Granddaddy J.D., and my great-grandmother, Grandma Lizzie, who lived just forty minutes away in Adams Run, South Carolina.

Their home and convenience store were central to that community. Locals frequented their store for groceries as well as a dose of camaraderie and laughter.

Granddaddy J.D. was a towering figure in our family—handsome, charismatic, and a master storyteller. People admired him not only for his work ethic and generosity but also for his ability to make everyone who entered his store feel valued. It was more than just a business; it was a gathering place, where community members could share their lives and connect with one another.

Grandma Lizzie played a crucial role in the store's success too. A kind woman with a warm spirit, she could win anyone over with her charm. Her legendary homemade Hoppin' John and corn bread attracted visitors from near and far, turning the convenience store into a beloved eatery. Even at eighty-five years old, she'd casually stroll to her chicken coop, grab a live chicken, and have a chicken dinner prepared in thirty minutes! She was old school, born in the late 1890s. Watching her interact with customers taught me valuable lessons about kindness and the positive impact it can have on communication.

Although we didn't live in Adams Run, we visited on weekends and holidays. The strong sense of family there helped ease my longing for my life in Germany. I quickly became a fan of Granddaddy J.D. He provided the kind of male attention young boys often crave. I looked forward to our trips to Adams Run, where the towering oak trees draped in Spanish moss enhanced the charm of my experiences. The time I spent in Adams Run allowed for reflection and connection. It was here I absorbed valuable life lessons from my wise family members, such as the importance of being a self-starter, respecting your elders, and always giving back to your community—lessons that would stay with me forever.

GRANDDADDY J.D.'S LESSONS IN LIFE

Granddaddy J.D. during the Korean War

Granddaddy J.D. was not just a pillar of support for my mother as she navigated the complexities of raising us on her own while my father faced financial struggles; he also played a crucial role in shaping my values and character. If I had to name only one influential figure in my life, it would undoubtedly be Granddaddy J.D. He transcended the typical role of a grandfather and became my mentor and role model. His guidance went beyond familial ties; he invested in my personal growth and taught me valuable lessons about responsibility and a strong work ethic.

Before my parents divorced, I had little understanding of money, but afterward, discussions about it became constant. This was the point in my life when I realized we didn't have a lot of money, and at the age of eight, I became anxious about my finances. I yearned for my granddad to show me how to earn it. My focus during visits to Adams Run shifted from playing with other kids to convincing him to assign me tasks he would pay me to perform around the store.

Finally, one day, Granddaddy J.D. obliged and took me on as a child laborer. My very first responsibilities included sweeping up and stocking the shelves. He paid me one dollar an hour, but I also had access to unlimited food and drink. He had a special fondness for me and enjoyed spending time with me more than he did with my brothers and cousins. He would often let me tell my mother how well behaved I was and that I could spend weekends with him in Adams Run. I cherished this attention and made the most of the opportunity; I am sure he enjoyed passing on his wisdom to a kid who was eager to learn.

Eventually, at the age of nine, I graduated to the cash register. It was a big step for me, a chance to take on more responsibility and learn about the world of finance, as well as negotiating tactics when folks attempted to barter with me. I remember standing on a stool behind the counter, my hands barely visible over the register, feeling accomplished and excited.

Looking back, that cash register was where I discovered my love for numbers, the intricacies of managing money, and that leaders in a community must also support that community when times are tough. I watched my granddad give away groceries at times due to job losses, divorces, and deaths in the family. Digital cash registers were not a thing back then, so handling all the transactions, counting the dollars and cents to ensure my register was balanced, made me excellent at math. I started thinking in numbers; it was this small job that sparked my fascination with both business and community support, lessons that have stayed with me.

I studied how my grandad dealt with customers until I could replicate his style of communication. His eyes beamed with pride and satisfaction whenever he saw me take on a customer and deal with them the way he would. "Boy, you learn fast, eh." He would pat me on the back and give me a five-dollar bill every time he felt I did something exceptional. His faith in me made me feel good about myself and inspired me to do my best.

Granddaddy J.D. firmly believed in being smart with money and always stressed the importance of saving and investing wisely. I had seen my father make poor choices with money all my life, so I knew how important it was to learn to manage my finances.

Granddaddy J.D. would share with me stories of his own experiences, his challenges, and the lessons he had learned about managing finances. "Always save for a rainy day," he would say, his voice filled with the wisdom of someone who had weathered many storms. "You never know when you might need it. Life is unpredictable, but you should be wise enough to prepare for the storms ahead."

He taught me to appreciate the value of a dollar and the importance of budgeting. Through his guidance, I learned how to set financial goals, plan for the future, and make informed decisions about spending and saving. His lessons were practical and insightful, providing me a foundation of financial literacy that has served me well throughout my life.

One of the most memorable lessons he taught me was about delayed gratification. He explained that the rewards of patience and perseverance often far outweigh the temporary satisfaction of impulsive spending. "Good things come to those who wait," he would say, encouraging me to prioritize long-term gains over short-term pleasures. This principle became a cornerstone of my financial philosophy, guiding my decisions and shaping my approach to money management.

Granddaddy J.D. also instilled in me the importance of generosity and giving back to the community. He believed financial success wasn't just about accumulating wealth; it was also about using that wealth to positively impact others. Watching him support local charities and lend a helping hand to those in need taught me the value of compassion and the power of giving.

I was devastated when he died of cancer due to Agent Orange exposure during the Korean War. At the age of fifty-nine, he was gone far too soon. During his final years, he called on my uncle to come train with him to take over the business, but my uncle refused to leave New York City. My mother would have been a viable option, given her accounting experience, but he didn't see her that way since she never took the time to help in the store.

Granddad's estate planning was a mess; he didn't trust banks. Because we were close, I knew he had a few hundred thousand dollars stuffed in his mattress when he died. Unfortunately, everything he had amassed was either stolen after his death or caught up in legal battles, leaving my mom with nothing. Despite this, his legacy lives on in the lessons he taught me. I saw it as my responsibility to build on those lessons, even if I was starting from the bottom.

BREAKING BARRIERS AND BELIEFS

One of my earliest experiences with victory was in fifth grade at Summerville Elementary School. When my English teacher announced the upcoming spelling bee, I was so eager to prove myself I immediately asked her to sign me up without even consulting my mother. When I eventually did tell my mom that I had entered, she acknowledged my enthusiasm and encouraged me to do my best as she hurried off to her second job. Supported or not, I was determined to win.

I immersed myself in studying to prepare for the spelling bee. "Boy, when do you plan on sleeping?" my great-grandmother, Bertha, would ask when she saw me sitting on her plastic-covered couch deep into the night, devouring spelling words. I often ignored her concerns.

Growing up in South Carolina had made me acutely aware of race, and I was motivated to prove to my classmates that despite being a person of color, I was at the top of my game when it came to spelling. My brothers laughed at me and called me a nerd, but I wasn't competing against them; I was competing against my friend Bill, who lived in a large house on the other side of town and was also determined to win.

Finally, the day of the competition arrived. It was an interschool event, and parents were not invited, which was a relief for me since my mom was busy with two or three jobs and couldn't have attended. The competition was a level playing field. I breezed through the preliminary rounds thanks to my hard work. The final round pitted me against Bill and a girl named Shelby, whom I had a crush on. I had to beat both of them!

The room was tense, filled with nervous breaths. The final word was announced: "gorgeous." My heart raced; it was a word I had practiced extensively. Bill misspelled it, and then Shelby followed suit. It was my turn.

Taking a deep breath, I closed my eyes for a moment to focus. The crowd disappeared as I visualized each letter in my mind. "G-O-R-G-E-O-U-S," I spelled out confidently, nailing the tricky parts effortlessly. The room erupted in applause from the teachers and students, and I was flooded with relief and exhilaration as I realized I had won.

The school principal approached holding a trophy symbolizing my victory that gleamed under the stage lights. However, the real prize was the portable AM/FM radio they presented next. It was sleek and state of the art, and it felt like a gateway to endless music on Z-93 and stories for my great-grandmother. I couldn't wait to show Mama Bertha the prize I had won for her.

When I got home, I rushed in, eager to share the news with Mama Bertha, a devout deaconess at our church and a woman I deeply admired. I expected a joyous, "Praise the Lord!" upon sharing my news. I headed straight to the kitchen, where the smell of freshly made peach cobbler filled the air. I found her sitting at the kitchen table, thick glasses perched on her nose as she flipped through her Bible.

"Mama Bertha, I won the spelling bee!" I exclaimed, placing the shiny trophy and radio on the table. She looked at both items, her facial expression shifting to a curious smile. But her response surprised me. "Well, there must not have been any white kids in that spelling bee," she said with a chuckle. "There's no way a little nukkah could win against them!"

For a moment, her words stung, leaving me speechless. My jaw dropped, and my eyes widened. I knew my class was mostly white, and I was the underdog, but surely she knew I could overcome the odds. Her comment hit me hard, but this was a woman who had spent her life as a nanny in the Deep South. She had photos of both Jesus and Ronald Reagan hanging in her living room. Though I was young, I understood her perspective, but I didn't let it diminish my joy.

Instead, I grinned and wrapped my arms around her. "Well, Mama Bertha, I just won you a brand-new radio!" I teased. She laughed at my resilience, patted me on the back, praised Jesus, and made me a bowl of peach cobbler with vanilla ice cream.

Later, I realized her reaction stemmed from her own history and experiences as someone who was only one generation removed from the institution of slavery in this country.

CUB SCOUT GLORY

Still living in Summerville, South Carolina, at seven years old at my great-grandparents' house, I had a burning desire to join the Cub Scouts since half my friends were involved in scouting. I longed to wear a uniform like my dad and granddad had in the military, and this was my opportunity. Being part of a troop, learning new skills, and embarking on adventures excited me more than anything else. After weeks of pleading and promising I would use my own money to join and I would be responsible, my mother finally gave in and let me sign up.

I was the only Black kid and the only scout without two married parents in my troop. On top of that, my brothers and Black classmates never missed an opportunity to tease me about it. They laughed and made jokes, calling me "Scout Boy," "Buckwheat," and "Whitey" and asking if I had earned my "cookie badge" yet. This was my first experience with the crab mentality, where people from the same social group try to pull down or undermine those trying to better themselves. Despite their teasing, I wore my uniform proudly and felt a sense of belonging in the Cub Scouts, even though I looked different from the rest of my troop.

The big event for the Cub Scouts in Summerville was the soapbox-car derby. This annual race, where participants raced homemade, gravity-powered cars down a hill, was the highlight of the scouting year. It was a thrilling event, and I was eager to showcase my creativity and racing skills in such a fun and competitive atmosphere.

What I failed to realize was that not having a dad around put me at a significant disadvantage. I quickly noticed most scouts had their dads helping them build their cars. It was a bonding experience for many of the boys and their fathers, sharing laughs and lessons in garages filled with the smell of sawdust and paint. My dad was in Germany, my Granddaddy J.D. was sick with cancer at the time, and my great-granddad was in his nineties and focused on delivering the word as a deacon. Therefore, I had no choice but to take on the challenge by myself.

With limited resources, I carved up my box car. I went into my mom's fingernail-polish drawer and swiped some red and blue polish. I was going to be patriotic if nothing else, dammit! I then attached some wheels and caught my great granddad as he was going inside to ask the deacon to pray for my car, which he did.

I won't lie; my car was not great. It smelled like nail polish, the frame was misaligned, and the wheels were wobbly, but I was proud of it. My brothers laughed heartily when they saw it, calling it a "hooptie" and a "crackhead mobile." I was excited to be part of the race, but I was also nervous about what the other kids and their dads would think of my car.

On race day, I brought my car to the starting line. The other cars were sleek and shiny, crafted with precision and expertise, while mine was held together with duct tape and the prayers of my great-grandfather, Deacon Chester Adams. I knew it might fall apart at any moment.

As the race began, I watched as the other cars sped ahead, their drivers leaning forward with determination. My car trailed behind, rattling and wobbling its way down the track. I came in last place, but my car survived the day, and a sense of joy filled me as I completed the challenge by myself. This experience taught me that grit and determination—even in defeat— can feel more rewarding than winning within your means.

Eventually, I had to drop out of Cub Scouts. The annual father–son camping trip was coming up, and I was the only one who would be attending with my mom. My mother committed to the trip, as I had worked hard to get to this point in my scouting career. She reluctantly packed our gear and even borrowed some camping equipment from neighbors to ensure we were prepared.

At the campsite, it quickly became clear we were the odd ones out. The other boys were there with their fathers, building campfires and bonding over stories of their adventures. My mother, who was a "girl's girl," definitely did not fit in with this group of avid anglers and outdoorsmen. We pitched a crooked tent, which a couple dads helped fix. Mom even joined in on some activities that first night, but I could tell she was miserable.

Despite her best efforts, it was obvious my mom was painfully out of her element. To make matters worse, there were dads who disapproved of her presence on a male bonding trip; they exchanged knowing glances and chuckled at her lack of camping expertise while their sons, my fellow scouts, whispered among themselves. I could sense my mother's discomfort, and although she tried to hide it, I knew this wasn't the experience I had hoped for. I told her I was okay with leaving, and we departed immediately.

After the camping trip, my mother sat me down with sadness in her eyes. She gently explained that she needed to step back from helping with my scouting and suggested I explore other activities where I could feel more included and supported. Though her words were soft, the deep pain of acknowledging her inadequacy as a father figure in my Cub Scout experience was evident in her expression.

Reflecting on my childhood experiences, I realize I learned early on the importance of resilience and perseverance. When my parents separated, I faced the difficult task of choosing between them and dealing with the absence of my father. Moving to South Carolina brought further challenges as I adjusted to a new school, home, and community.

These experiences taught me that life doesn't pause for anyone, and the only way forward is to keep moving. Despite my early difficulties and uncertainty, I learned to adapt to new environments and embrace change as an opportunity for growth.

CHAPTER 1 TRIGGERS

Reflecting on my broken path, it is clear how my childhood experiences shaped my ability to cope and grow despite challenges.

- The trauma of my parents' divorce at a young age left me feeling insecure and abandoned. Constantly moving and adapting to new places intensified my sense of uncertainty and anxiety.
- My father's extreme discipline and high demands created tension and impacted my self-worth, while his absence left a void that was difficult to fill.
- Adjusting to life in South Carolina brought about a significant cultural and environmental shift, triggering homesickness and a feeling of displacement.
- Facing racial and social challenges, such as being the only Black kid in my Cub Scout troop and dealing with teasing from my brothers and Black friends, added to feelings of exclusion and the need to prove myself, resulting in isolation.
- Financial anxiety became a part of my life after my parents' divorce, leading me to understand the importance of earning money and managing finances.
- The loss of my grandfather, Granddaddy J.D., was a devastating blow, and navigating his estate planning issues further heightened my sense of financial insecurity.

Despite these formidable challenges, I discovered ways to adapt and grow. While my experiences in the Cub Scouts were tough, they instilled in me the values of grit and determination. Embracing change as an opportunity for growth and persisting through headwinds became my strengths.

Through it all, I cultivated resilience, mastering the ability to navigate life's obstacles and derive strength from my experiences. This journey imparted valuable lessons on perseverance, adaptability, and the significance of maintaining hope and determination in the face of adversity.

CHAPTER 2

EXTRA! EXTRA!

IT'S STRANGE HOW THE IDEA OF FAIRNESS WE HOLD IN OUR minds rarely matches the reality we live in. Our textbooks teach us about a completely different world—a place where everyone is given a chance, a sanctuary where each person is searching for peace. Yet, the real world is vastly different.

For years, I watched my mother return home from work with a tired smile, hoping to get a few hours of rest before getting ready for her second or third job. She would hang up her coat, kick off her shoes, call a girlfriend or two, and settle into the predictable rhythm of getting ready for the next shift. She lived for the weekends, when she typically only worked one job and had time to spend with her children and for herself.

I can honestly say I did not feel we, as growing boys, were better off without my father, even if he was a man of intense control who rarely loosened his grip. There was a period when my brothers and I were true latchkey kids after we moved out of my great-grandparents' home and into our own. There was more space, but now Mom had to work even harder to keep the lights on and food on the table, especially as there was no longer any money coming in from Granddaddy J.D., whose health continued to decline during this time.

As I mentioned earlier, my mom and dad loved each other, but it was the kind of love that came with rules. Mom couldn't go out after work—not to a friend's house, not even to a café for a quick cup of tea. Home was supposed to be where she belonged, but ironically, it also became her prison.

Many people do not realize how serious mental abuse is. My mom left because my dad's control was suffocating. They were both very young, and I am confident neither of them truly understood what they were doing, especially with three kids to care for. Arguments would often erupt over the most trivial things. For instance, my dad hated soup, so to spite him, my mom would make it, resulting in an argument. Even tone of voice could quickly spark a heated exchange. These disputes were always deeper than they seemed; they revolved around dominance, illustrating my mother's relentless struggle to assert her individuality in the shadow of my father's unyielding control.

I sat there, a silent witness to it all. I was too young to fully grasp the complexities of their relationship but not too young to be spared the sting of injustice. This was my first real lesson in how life works—or, more accurately, how it doesn't. I learned that life isn't fair. It doesn't offer everyone the same freedom, opportunities, or respect, even within a family unit.

My mother was a resilient woman, yet she longed to break free from the constraints of a stifling marriage that choked her. Witnessing her endure the repetitive pattern of conflicts and silent struggles, I came to understand that true strength was not the same as fairness. It wasn't solely about deserving better or working harder. Sometimes, it boiled down to power—who held the keys to freedom and who was left to futilely rattle the cage.

THE STRUGGLES OF A SINGLE MOTHER

Life in Summerville was okay, or at least as fine as it could be after my mother separated from my father. A quite peace settled over the house. My mom, though small in frame and stature, continued to hold down at least two jobs to shore up her finances and provide for us.

I remember those early days after moving into our own home vividly;

several years had passed since we'd left Germany, and I was now ten years old. My two brothers and I were quickly growing into adolescents. My older brother was twelve, already feeling the pull of teenage rebellion, while my younger brother, who was seven, still clung to the last threads of his childhood innocence. We were three extremely active boys who ran circles around our tiny mother.

Mom tried her best to manage the chaos that came with raising three boys. She offered us guidance, and when we were truly in trouble, she attempted to spank us. However, her spankings had little effect as we often hit each other harder while wrestling with our friends, trying to emulate the top wrestlers of our day, like Ric Flair and the Four Horsemen. It wasn't long before the strain of raising us began to show. Parenting three boys is no small feat, especially alone.

She did everything she could, but deep down, I think she knew there was no way she could handle us as we started pushing against the limits.

My older brother began running with the wrong crowd. In one particularly egregious instance of youthful rebellion that stands out in my memory, he took one of my mom's friends' cars for a joyride. He was trying to maintain a certain image, which led to fights at school and my mom having to leave work to pick him up.

The incident that likely broke the camel's back was when a classmate of my older brother got in trouble for stealing from a store. This classmate gave my brother's name at the police station, and my mom had to go there, only to find she had no idea who this kid was. This incident quickly made my mother realize she was losing control.

If she had no other choice but to do it alone, I'm sure she would have, but we had a father. At times, he would call and lecture us; he was still present in our lives, and my mom knew he could help get us back in line. She felt we needed a drill sergeant, so a decision was made without input from my brothers or me.

WELCOME HOME, PRIVATE RITTER

We were never told outright that we were going to live with our dad. There were no serious discussions or heart-to-heart talks about what this change would mean for us. Instead, it was framed as a simple weekend trip. "You're going to stay with your father this weekend," my mom said. He had just returned from Germany, and he was now a drill sergeant at Fort Knox in Kentucky. We didn't think much of it; after all, we hadn't spent significant time with our dad in a while, so a weekend with him sounded great. But as we headed down the highway, something felt different. The air was thicker, and I noticed my mother had been unusually quiet before we left. She also packed our bags with a certain finality, tucking away more clothes than we normally would have needed for a two-day visit.

I remember that weekend vividly—the smell of my father's Polo cologne when he came to pick us up. We didn't realize it then, but this was no ordinary weekend. It was the beginning of something new, something we hadn't been prepared for. We were now going to live with our father, and I felt extremely betrayed that my parents hadn't even discussed it with us beforehand.

As I mentioned earlier, my father was now a drill sergeant—a man of rigid discipline and little concern for domestic comforts. He had spent the last few years as a bachelor, and his house—sorry, I mean trailer—reflected that in every sense. Moving from my mom's place, which was a modest but stable middle-class home in South Carolina, to my dad's broken-down trailer park in Radcliffe, Kentucky, felt like stepping into a different world. A huge boulder of reality struck my brothers and me with full force, and there was nothing that could have shielded us from its impact. It wasn't just the peeling paint on the walls or the creaky floorboards that told me things were different. The cold, hard truth that we were broke and now under my dad's discipline absolutely crushed my spirit. Every inch of the trailer screamed we were in for a new chapter, and we had no choice but to accept our fate.

The trailer was small, cramped, and far from what we were used to. We felt some relief when our dad told us it was a temporary solution while we waited for on-base housing to become available. But when you're living in a trailer in Radcliffe, Kentucky, "temporary" feels like forever. My dad had my older brother and me make that trailer immaculate. We even used toothbrushes to clean spots on the carpet. To this day, I am a stickler for cleanliness thanks to my dad's relentless campaign of washing and scrubbing. My dad did not want to hear complaints about the trailer. For him, we had one job: keep it clean. We had a roof over our heads, so we needed to make the most of it—nothing more, nothing less.

The size of the trailer was a joke; it was never meant to accommodate three growing boys. I slept on the couch with my younger brother for what felt like an eternity. It wasn't even a proper couch, more of a lumpy, old thing that sagged in the middle, with faded upholstery that had long lost its color. But it became my bed. Every night, I'd stretch out as much as I could, trying to find comfort amid the springs poking at my back. Privacy was a luxury my younger brother and I did not have. We were on top of each other, elbows bumping, his feet in my face as I tried to sleep. The one positive was that it brought my brother and me really close together, and it was during this time that I started looking out for him more.

During those days and nights in the trailer, I often thought back to my mom's house—the decorations, the sense of care she put into making it feel like a home. In my new environment, there was no warmth, no softness. My dad's version of love was different. It was practical, tough, and a bit rough around the edges. He believed that as long as we had food to eat, a place to sleep, and clothes on our backs, the rest didn't matter. The three of us were a package; if one of us acted up, we all suffered the consequences. The deal made between my parents was clear: going back to my mom's was out of the question.

LIFE IN MY DAD'S WORLD

In the beginning, when we first arrived at my dad's house, we had decent contact with my mom. She would mail us letters and call occasionally. For birthdays and holidays, she would send small amounts of money our way, which made a significant difference to us. With that money, we would buy name-brand shoes and other things we needed to help us keep up with what other kids were wearing to school. It provided a sense of normalcy, a lifeline that kept us from completely sinking into the reality of our desperate situation.

I remember the first time a package arrived, tucked inside a worn-out envelope with my mom's careful handwriting scrawled across the front. The money inside felt like a piece of her—her way of supporting us even when she couldn't be there physically. It wasn't much, but it meant we didn't have to rely entirely on what little my dad could spare. We could breathe a little easier, if only for a moment.

During this time with my father, my beloved Granddaddy J.D. lost his battle with cancer and passed away. This was the lowest point in my young life, and I knew it would wipe out the financial support we'd been receiving from my mom. The letters and gifts from her stopped completely after we buried Granddaddy. I was still young but old enough to understand that things were about to get a lot tougher. With no more envelopes arriving in the mail and no safety net to catch us when things got hard, I didn't fully grasp it then, but our circumstances had shifted. The little comfort we had was gone.

That was when life began to stare me in the eye, unblinking and relentless. There was no buffer anymore, no one to fall back on. Every day was a reminder that we were on our own now—just my dad, my brothers, and me. The things I had taken for granted before—a new pair of shoes when mine wore out, clothes that fit properly—were no longer coming in. It was rough.

I remember driving into Fort Knox from Radcliffe once to help my dad repair his car, and the difference between the base and where we were living was striking. The base housing looked like mansions to my brothers and me. The homes were well kept, the streets were clean, and there was a sense of order that was nonexistent in the trailer park. Everything there seemed structured, organized, and a bit more refined. It made me wonder why we weren't living there, especially knowing that my father, as a drill sergeant, could have easily secured a spot on base.

I knew many of my dad's peers lived on the base with their families, and I was determined to move there by any means necessary. I looked forward to the day when I wouldn't have to dwell in a run-down trailer in Radcliffe with peeling wallpaper and floors that creaked under every step. I longed for a room with a real bed and a home with enough space that it didn't feel like my brothers and I were always breathing down each other's necks.

I asked my dad about moving onto the base a couple times, but he was not happy with my questions, so I decided it was best for my health to stay away from the topic.

The situation perplexed me. Maybe it was stubbornness, maybe it was pride, or maybe he had his own reasons I was too young to understand. As I have grown older, I've come to speculate that part of the reason we spent a year in that trailer living off base was so my dad could keep his freedom of movement and maintain some distance between the military and his personal life.

I have also since learned that the military pays you a stipend to live off post that increases with each dependent. Gaining three boys, my dad's revenue increased, but his expenses for rent stayed the same. Had he moved on post, his stipend would have disappeared. This realization shed new light on his reluctance to discuss our living situation and underscored the complexities that shaped my family's situation during that time.

THESE PAPERS WON'T SELL THEMSELVES

It wasn't long before I started to feel the pinch, especially when it came to necessities like school clothes and supplies. I didn't want to keep asking my dad for what little he could spare; depending on his mood, I might get a couple dollars or I might be yelled at. I quickly realized the 20 percent chance of gaining a few dollars was not worth the risk, especially when 80 percent of the time, my dad unleashed fury on me. I would rather be broke than go through that.

I was in fifth grade then, but I could feel my grandfather watching over me, encouraging me to find a way to earn some money myself. That's how I ended up becoming a paperboy.

It all started when I noticed a couple kids from the neighborhood, close to my age, piling into a plain, white ice-cream truck early in the mornings before school. They would come in through the side door, and watching them hop onto the truck piqued my curiosity. At first, I didn't think much of it, but as the weeks passed, I noticed those kids had nice school clothes. I needed to find out if this had anything to do with the truck they boarded every morning.

One afternoon, while playing marbles in the dusty yard outside the trailers, I had a chance encounter that changed everything. I was a skilled marble player, always willing to bet a few quarters or win the other player's prized marbles in a game. When two kids from the truck approached, I knew I could win some money and marbles from these high rollers. As I pocketed their money and marbles, I struck up a conversation. I casually asked where they went every morning. One of the boys, fingers still dusty from the game, looked at me and grinned. "We're selling papers on the military base," he said. I must have looked surprised because he laughed, and the others joined in, sharing stories about their early-morning escapades outside the mess hall—where soldiers eat—selling newspapers to basic-training soldiers as they rushed back to their barracks for morning duties.

As I listened, something clicked inside me. *This could be my chance*, I thought. If they could do it, why couldn't I? I needed money—not just for myself but for my family too. My brothers and I could finally update our school clothes, and I wanted to buy a few things I had gone without for too long. After hearing them out, I asked if they could help me get in. "Can you introduce me to the guy in charge?" I asked. The boys nodded in agreement, and one of them mentioned he could put in a good word for me. That was all I needed to hear.

The gentleman in charge of paper delivery was an older man named Lee Busroll. He was a gruff, no-nonsense guy in his sixties, a retired sergeant who had started this paper route to supplement his retirement while being his own boss. When I finally met Lee, I told him I was 100 percent willing to meet him at 6:00 a.m. every morning, no matter the weather, to sell newspapers. Lee could sense my eagerness, and he hired me on the spot. I was assigned my post outside the mess hall, where the new trainees lined up for meals.

This job was definitely not glamorous, and it wasn't salaried; it was all about sales. If you didn't sell any papers, you didn't make any money. Make no mistake, newspapers do not sell themselves to seventeen-to-twenty-year-olds; the client needed to be convinced. That said, I felt a strange sense of pride standing there, clutching a stack of newspapers that smelled of fresh ink and anticipation. The mess hall was a large, brick building, a bit imposing with its worn-down exterior and the steady stream of soldiers marching in and out like clockwork. On the first day of my new job, I stood outside the heavy double doors, my feet planted on the cold pavement, and watched the line of soldiers approach.

I waited, scanning their faces for any flicker of interest, any sign they might reach for a paper. Five soldiers passed me, showing no interest. However, I was determined not to let this opportunity slip away. When the sixth soldier came out, I mustered up my courage and called out softly, "Paper, sir?" At first, my voice was too quiet, getting lost in the noise of shuffling boots and barked military orders. But I persisted.

"Paper, sir?!" I repeated, my words becoming stronger and louder. It felt strange calling out to young men who towered over me, their faces hardened from the hazing of drill sergeants during hours of training, their minds focused on the next drill or exercise. Some soldiers would glance down at me upon hearing my voice and toss a few coins my way without a word, their eyes barely registering my presence as they grabbed a paper and hurried inside. Others would pause for a moment, look me over, and then crack a small smile before taking a paper and nodding their thanks. Those moments felt like tiny victories.

The weather was as fierce as the training these privates endured. In winter, the cold was a relentless adversary. It seemed to penetrate every layer of my clothing, seeping into my bones as the biting wind howled across the base. My fingers, numb and stiff, would struggle to grip the newspapers, and my breath would form frosty clouds in the air. I'd shuffle from foot to foot, trying to keep warm on the icy pavement. The cold would nip at my cheeks and make my voice sound like it was coming from an icebox when I called out, "Paper, sir?!"

The summer was no easier but in a different way. The sweltering heat would turn the air into a heavy, oppressive blanket. Sweat would bead on my forehead and trickle down my back, soaking my clothes and making them cling uncomfortably to my skin. The sun would blaze down, turning the asphalt into a scorching surface that seemed to radiate heat back at me. Every call of "Paper, sir!" felt like a struggle against the oppressive warmth that drained my energy with each passing minute.

As I stood there day after day—rain, snow, or shine—I began to learn the rhythms of the soldiers: how they walked, how they carried themselves, and the weary look in their eyes after a long day of training. I wasn't just there to sell papers; I was observing the sacrifices the soldiers were making to better themselves. I was sacrificing as well!

PAPERBOY MARKETING 101

My job as a paperboy was more than just standing at my post; it was about timing and strategy. I had to catch the moment between when a private exited the mess hall, eyes glazed with exhaustion, and when they hurried back to the barracks to focus on the next training task. I would station myself outside the large mess hall, knowing every second counted. On weekdays, I stood firm at 6:15 a.m. as the crowd of tired soldiers shuffled out after their meal. On weekends, the routine was even earlier; I would drag myself out of bed before the sun, arriving at 5:30 a.m. to greet the first wave of early risers.

I offered the local paper for thirty-five cents and *USA Today* for fifty cents, and each sale earned me a modest five-cent cut. It wasn't much, but it was something. The real profit, though, came from those hurried privates who, in their rush to get back to their routines or because they were nice guys, would hand over a dollar bill without waiting for change. Those moments led me to realize that there was more to this job than just selling newspapers; I needed to form a relationship with these guys to increase my chances of getting a tip.

True success would not come from simply waving the papers around, saying, "Paper, sir." I needed to market myself better. I quickly ascertained that if I stood passively, I could sell a decent amount of papers, but at a nickel-a-piece commission, a good day was eight dollars if you added in several tips, and a great day was twelve dollars—to do either, I needed to sell at least one hundred newspapers.

To boost my sales and tips, I learned to inject a bit of flair into my pitch—calling out with enthusiasm, sharing sports scores, teasing Brooke Shields or Whitney Houston news, anything to get a half-second glance from these guys. I pitched the papers in a way that made them seem indispensable, stressing that they needed to know what was going on back home or with the Cold War. I strived to create an urgency that made them feel like the news was a must-have rather than a mere option. It was about making every newspaper feel like a vital piece of the world they were missing out on.

As I mentioned earlier, one of the valuable lessons I learned from my Granddaddy J.D. was the importance of being friendly and building strong connections with customers. He had a way of making everyone feel important, a skill I admired and aspired to emulate. When I started selling newspapers at Fort Knox, I carried this lesson with me, applying it to every interaction I had on the base.

From the very beginning, I made it a point to establish a rapport with the various people in charge—the mess-hall staff and drill sergeants. I greeted everyone with a smile, always polite and respectful. I would even give the most influential folks free newspapers, as I knew the relationships this gesture could build would pay me back several times over. I did not know what strategy was at that age, but the approach I took was strategic. It ensured my presence was welcomed and appreciated.

A few months into my job, the staff on post had become so fond of me, they would help me with my sales and encourage me as I braved the harsh weather.

My initial time as a paperboy taught me about perseverance, strategy, and the power of human connection. As I reflect on those days of braving the elements and engaging with the military community, I cherish the growth and memories that shaped me into a resilient and resourceful individual.

LESSONS FROM LEE

As the months passed, the drill sergeants began to recognize me, and this recognition translated to increased sales. On paydays, the first and fifteenth of each month, I quickly sold my papers and made an average of $100 to $150—no other paperboy was bringing in this much. My rapport with influential figures on the base was a significant factor in my success. The mess-hall staff and drill sergeants developed an affection for me and my work ethic, wanting to see me succeed. This newfound support made my job easier and more enjoyable.

Additionally, I discovered that my talent for rap, particularly battle rap, was a hit with the drill sergeants. They would invite me to the barracks to engage in rap battles with privates nearing graduation from basic training. I would show up with my papers, sell them all immediately, and then spend the next few hours in verbal contests with select soldiers. What started as just a job evolved into something much more fulfilling.

My reputation as a successful paperboy grew, drawing the attention of friends and family. My brothers and I enjoyed new clothes, and occasionally, we even bypassed the free school-cafeteria food for the much-tastier items for sale. This became a remarkable recruitment method for new paperboys, leading to a wait list of kids eager to join the organization. In hindsight, it is surreal to think that at age ten, I took on a job to help my dad pay bills and buy school clothes and supplies for my brothers. My mindset was no different from that of a kid in the inner city who doesn't have a Lee Busroll to work for legally.

As Lee's sales, fueled by the efforts of myself and other top sellers, soared, he bought himself a new delivery truck and retired the ice-cream truck. He introduced a monthly "top sales" plaque to encourage competition among his paperboys. As his number-one salesperson, I was honored to ride up front with Lee ten out of twelve months. Lee's wisdom and guidance became a part of my life, and we became like family.

However, not everything was sweet. I learned a hard lesson about human nature and jealousy. Some around me seemed more interested in complaining about my success than in putting in their own effort. They resented my position as the top salesperson, viewing my achievements as a roadblock to their own success rather than as inspiration. Lee reminded me that throughout life, I would meet people with insecurities about the successes of others. These individuals, unwilling to confront their shortcomings, often undermine themselves in their quest for advancement. This revelation was eye-opening and shaped my perspective on competition and success.

CHAPTER 2 TRIGGERS

During this time, I developed several triggers that significantly impacted my life.

- Witnessing my parents' tumultuous relationship, characterized by arguments and emotional abuse, instilled in me feelings of helplessness and a mistrust in relationships.
- The lack of fairness and power imbalance in my parents' dynamic while they were married shaped my understanding of control and autonomy. Additionally, being sent to live with my father without any discussion left me feeling betrayed and powerless, fostering emotions of abandonment and resentment.
- The harsh living conditions and sudden loss of comfort following the transition to my father's run-down trailer evoked feelings of inadequacy and emotional instability within me. Taking on the responsibility of earning money at a young age to support my family led to stress and a loss of childhood innocence, instilling in me a constant need to prove my worth through hard work.
- The loss of maternal support after my grandfather's death deepened my feelings of isolation and abandonment, reinforcing the notion that I had to fend for myself without a safety net.
- My strained relationship with my father, his focus on practicality over comfort, and his lack of emotional warmth created a challenging environment where I felt unable to express my concerns or needs.
- Experiencing jealousy and competition as the top paperboy heightened my sensitivity to criticism and trust issues.
- The significant emotional blow of losing my beloved Granddaddy J.D. left me grappling with feelings of sadness, loneliness, and instability.

This chapter illuminated myriad emotional and environmental triggers that likely shaped my mental-health journey, contributing to long-term issues such as anxiety, trust challenges, emotional suppression, and a heightened need for control and self-reliance.

Recognizing and understanding these triggers was a crucial step in addressing their impact on me and paving the way for healing and growth in the future.

CHAPTER 3

AN UPHILL CLIMB

The early middle school years. I'm front row, second from right.

Fast-forwarding a couple years, my dad, my brothers, and I left Fort Knox, Kentucky, when the army transferred my dad to Mannheim, Germany. I was thrilled to be back in Germany, living on post full-time with access to new friends. However, I had a major issue: I had become a chubby kid due to my love for honey buns, Kool-Aid, and video games, all of which my paperboy job funded.

As my last act in Fort Knox, my classmates cast me as Fat Albert in a play. Fortunately, I had not yet gone through puberty, so I didn't fully comprehend how embarrassed I should have been. Now settled in Germany, I was starting sixth grade, and I realized the central locations of the kids and facilities on the military base meant I could get involved in sports.

At the time, I was overweight, but I wasn't going to let that stand in the way of my dreams. I signed up for the middle school intramural football league, where they promptly assigned me number seventy-seven and told me I would be a right guard. I had hoped to be a receiver, running back, or linebacker, so I had to swallow my pride, take my jersey, and get ready to play offensive line that year.

Playing on the offensive line was tough, and I admit it made me more rugged. However, I still dreamed of scoring touchdowns. My dad had been an all-state sprinter in high school, so I knew there was a fast kid inside me waiting to come out. After the season ended, I became determined to gain muscle and speed, so I started spending time at the gym, playing basketball, and lifting weights. I also rode my bike and walked all over Germany, even off base at times. Then, as if nature decided to give me a helping hand, I hit a growth spurt. It was a unique transition; one moment, I was an overweight kid, and the next, I had developed a decent athletic build almost overnight.

With my new build, my passion for sports soared. At the time, I wasn't quite athletic enough to be the star on any team's roster, but I managed to make the cut in a few sports. Over time, football emerged as my true passion; it was the one sport where I actually received significant playing time. The exhilaration I felt executing a perfect tackle on an opponent in my outside-linebacker position fueled my competitive spirit. I had so much to prove that I ended up shattering my ankle during an Oklahoma drill.

This drill—now banned—was a high-intensity physical exercise used in football practices. It consisted of a one-on-one tackling scenario where players went head-to-head to showcase their strength and physicality. The issue wasn't the drill itself; it was that I was the only player on the team who volunteered to face off against Conrad, the star of our team, a huge Samoan kid who had the physique of a twenty-year-old. The result of that drill for me was a shattered ankle. Even though I was injured for the remainder of the season, I earned a lot of respect that day. It was probably the first time my older brother showed me respect for anything physical, and it left me craving more.

Additionally, playing sports prompted me to think seriously about high school and life beyond it, particularly college. I knew several adults in my family who attended college, most of whom went to historically Black colleges and universities (HBCUs), but many either failed to graduate or weren't using the degrees they earned. I was fortunate to have an older cousin—Uyon—who was admitted to the prestigious Northwestern University. Everyone praised her intelligence, and I desired the same respect she received from the family; her achievements sparked a fire in me.

Uyon was not only brilliant, she also worked hard, which earned her a scholarship to an elite private high school called Seven Hills in Cincinnati, Ohio. In contrast, I hadn't attended any private schools. I changed schools every year and a half, and nobody even considered such an option for me at the time. My brothers and I were often overlooked due to the instability our parents inflicted on us through their constant moves and transitions. Nevertheless, dreams are free, and the limitations others set for me did not stop me from wanting to be the next Uyon.

I wanted to break out of the mold others had put me in and do something to redefine what was possible for me, but I had no clue how to accomplish that. I would lie awake at night, imagining the life I could have. I wanted to be debt-free, drive a nice car, have money in the bank, vacation once a year, and earn respect. The dream was quite simple, but I knew it would take hard work to achieve.

In my early teens, I had a consistent nightmare. In this dream, I couldn't move and was stuck in time. The clock ticked down to the deadline for submitting my college application, but I couldn't finish it, put it in an envelope, or send it off. In the end, I felt crushed, seeing myself delivering newspapers for the rest of my life. This nightmare kept me motivated to remain active in several extracurriculars at once. One day, my younger brother asked me why I was always stressed about school.

I replied that I stressed because I didn't want to struggle for the rest of my life. I observed how some of my friends lived, and I believed I could achieve a similar lifestyle if I kept pushing. I explained to him that I sought motivation everywhere, believing we can go wherever we want. As I shared this with him, I saw his mind working, contemplating the significance of not giving up. Conversations like these deepened our connection and strengthened our bond. I hoped to show him that persistence is not just about reaching goals but also about realizing the inner strength we all have to chase our dreams.

THE NEW BIG BRO

If someone had asked me what my superpower was in those days, I would have confidently said it was the "power of hope." As I entered my teenage years, life became increasingly tumultuous. The allure of being a gangster was very strong for many suburban kids in the late 1980s and early 1990s. Influenced by rap groups like N.W.A and movies such as *Scarface* and *Goodfellas*, everyone seemed to want to be the bad guy.

Reflecting on that time, I now find it odd that military kids in Germany were also acting out and rebelling. In eighth grade, I found myself at a crossroads: On one hand, I wanted to excel in the classroom; on the other hand, I was acutely aware that the "bad boys" were getting all the attention from girls. Another significant change took place during this time: My brother Ronald, known for his toughness, was leaving Germany to return to our mother in South Carolina.

Ronald, who didn't normally start fights but wouldn't back down from one either, defeated a high school junior in a fistfight when he was a freshman. The problem was that the high school junior's father was a colonel and my father's brigade commander. As a result, my father had no choice but to send my brother back to our mom to protect his career. It was the only logical choice in that situation. While Ronald wasn't always my protector, his presence served as a deterrent to others who may have otherwise sought a confrontation with me. We had a rule: If you fought one of us, you fought both of us. Even if you caught one of us alone, the other would be along eventually to help avenge his brother.

With Ronald gone, I felt the weight of being the older brother responsible for my younger brother, who now looked up to me. The dynamics in our house shifted dramatically after Ronald's departure. My dad's focus had always been on him, and his existence shielded me from many of my dad's ups and downs since they had much in common. I was often too opinionated for my dad, which didn't always go over well, and now that Ronald was gone, he would be dealing with me more often.

I had no choice but to grow up faster than I already was and embrace the responsibility of being the new big brother—the first one my dad would turn to when he wanted something done. I also had to figure out how to navigate my new role in the neighborhood. In that moment of upheaval, I knew I had to reinvent myself, and my journey of self-discovery truly began.

ADULTS CAN BE KIDS TOO

I was a year behind my brother in school, which meant his reputation became my shadow. His conflicts became mine, and I had to navigate through them. While issues with other kids were solvable, dealing with the adults was the real challenge.

I remember the looks I received from teachers the first day I walked into my second-semester eighth-grade classes. They all would look at me, then at my name, and back at me, narrowing their eyes as if bracing themselves for trouble. I could almost hear their thoughts: *This one's going to be a handful*. It wasn't a nice feeling.

That was when I realized adults can sometimes be worse than children. Some teachers, unfamiliar with who my brother and I were, made the choice not to be welcoming based on what they had heard in the teacher's lounge. There was one particular teacher, a retired sergeant major, who had a strong dislike for me right from the start. From the moment I walked into his classroom on the first day, I could tell from his expression that he had already made up his mind about me. He crossed his arms and stared me down as I found my seat. "I hope you're not planning on giving me trouble, young man," he said, looking over his glasses, his voice dripping with skepticism.

I looked up at him and tried to keep my tone even. "No, sir," I replied, but I could tell he didn't believe me. To him, I was guilty of a crime I hadn't yet committed, but he was sure I would. What frustrated me most about this teacher was that he was an elderly Black man who could have taught me valuable life lessons. Unfortunately, he chose to pick on a thirteen-year-old instead. This experience helped me realize that just because someone shares my racial or ethnic background does not mean they have my best interest at heart or will support me.

Dealing with the adults that semester was incredibly frustrating. I spent those first few months constantly trying to prove myself. It felt impossible to earn an A when the teacher was inclined to give me a C at best. My grades, regardless of my performance, seemed predetermined. All I could do was work hard, keep my head down, and do my best.

One particular moment still stands out in my memory. Our math teacher was going over a problem on the board when he turned around and asked, "Does anyone know the answer?" I raised my hand, surprising him. He called on me, probably expecting me to get it wrong. Instead, I explained the solution clearly, and he paused, looking at me with new-found respect.

"Hmm," he muttered, scratching his head. "That was unexpected." Although my grades didn't reflect my efforts that year, I had other things on my mind as I worked through the adjustment.

THE PROTÉGÉ

Life without my older brother had become stable. My grades were below my standard, and school was frustrating me, so I turned more to the gym and lifting weights. The gym became my favorite place because I could build myself up, not just physically but mentally. The more I worked out, the more I felt myself changing, and my personality began to evolve. At the same time, girls who had just been faces in the hallways started to catch my attention in ways they hadn't before. I would strategically place myself in the middle of the hallway against some other kids' lockers just to make eye contact. This is when I became acutely aware of how I presented myself.

My home life always engulfed in a whirlwind of change, my dad had remarried in Germany, and he and his wife now had a baby. Whether true or not, it seemed like my brother and I became an afterthought; it was probably the way it had to be given the commitment a new baby and marriage require.

I never complained. I enjoyed the freedom that came with the situation. Now, I had the power to stay out as late as I wanted. However, the financial situation at home was tighter than ever, and if I had any hope of getting a girlfriend, I needed to step up my fashion game. The military brats in Germany were ruthless when it came to making fun of people's clothes and ostracizing them. The fashion police roamed Mannheim, Germany, 24/7.

To support my younger brother and help with household bills, I got a job bagging groceries at the commissary (the military grocery store). Like my previous paperboy job, this position relied heavily on tips and relationships, so I did what was necessary to quickly become a top earner. Most of the guys working at the commissary were high schoolers looking to go to college or enter the military after graduation. These were not the guys who aspired to be the next Scarface.

It was interesting to get a glimpse into how things worked in high school as an eighth grader. The guys making money from bagging groceries could barely get a date, while those pretending to be Scarface had bustling social lives and tons of admirers. I paid attention to this as I wanted both, but realistically, I knew I was only getting the grocery-bag money.

In retrospect, that period of my life was marked by significant growth, self-discovery, and pain. Even though I used my earnings from bagging groceries to support my brother and myself, I always tried to make the outside world believe my family life was great. I earned just enough to maintain this facade. I was also a few years into football, which helped me make friends.

The most impactful friendship I had during this time was with a guy named David Moore. David was African American and German. One of the coolest aspects of his life was his mom, who was German and the nicest person I had ever met. She adored her three sons and their friends, and his house became a place where I could experience the motherly love I didn't have in my home at the time.

David and I started out as video game nerds, but then he hit a huge growth spurt that made him the best athlete and most sought-after guy in middle school. I became his protégé, still managing the video games, but by default, I became a "cool kid." This was something I desperately needed, especially since teachers were stopping me from being great. As a result, I decided to focus on having fun the year before high school. I was mature enough to understand what needed to be done once I entered ninth grade.

Prior to David's growth spurt, I was never popular for anything. If you have ever watched *The Wire*, I was a middle school version of Proposition Joe. I was the guy who could sell you some candy, negotiate comic book trades, give you the latest Nintendo game code, or deliver your pants to Mic Conteh so he could airbrush them. I was the first one to know the cheat code: up, up, down, down, left, right, left, right, B, A, start. However, I eventually became associated with the cool kids. This required me to get a few snap-in gold teeth, a New York Knicks Starter jacket, and a money clip.

The jacket, the hat, the gold—these things were certainly an affront to my true self. The math nerd was still inside, waiting to come back out.

THE FIGHT FOR RESPECT

I was still dreaming of attending college, but my teachers disillusioned me that year. Engaging in all that "cool kid" behavior was merely a fleeting attempt at gaining attention. It quickly dawned on me that aligning with the popular crowd meant becoming a target for those who would seek social capital by messing with the perceived weakest member of the popular group. As a result, I found myself having to defend myself on several occasions.

The occasion I recall most vividly involved a kid named Datillio. He was quite large and made my life miserable. To save face, I often snuck out the back door of the school to avoid him.

One day, in class, he backhanded me so hard my glasses flew across the room. I had two choices: (1) fall into obscurity or (2) face the bully on the battlefield. I opted for the battlefield, and we agreed to meet on the concrete pathway outside the school. My strategy was simple: hold him off for three to five minutes until an adult broke up the fight. A draw or even a slight loss would be a victory for me.

So there we were, surrounded by what seemed like the entire school, facing off. I was trying to look tough, but I was about to wet myself. The bully was furious—no one ever challenged him; how dare I? He charged at me. I stepped aside and managed to land a couple punches to his face. He rushed to grab me, but I kneed him and wrestled away, and we began to circle each other. He finally got ahold of me and slammed me to the hard concrete. I did everything I could to avoid tapping out for what felt like an eternity. Eventually, a few high schoolers broke up the fight. I didn't win, but I didn't lose either. I managed to get through the rest of eighth grade and half of ninth grade without any further fights.

My bravery had far better results than I could have ever hoped. I even got to date one of the most popular girls in my class for four days before she dumped me for a high schooler. Regardless of everything going on around me, I stayed true to myself. I didn't bully others; I refused to compromise my values for popularity. Besides, I was still trying to find my place at home amid the tumult of my dad and his new wife.

Time passed, and I moved on to high school in ninth grade. I was once again at the bottom of the social ladder. However, with new teachers, my love for school reemerged, and I started excelling academically. The teachers supported me, and I worked hard to achieve good grades.

Just as I settled into ninth grade in Germany, my dad received military orders to relocate to Fort Carson, Colorado. This was the worst possible timing as football season had just started. I now had to pick myself up and move to Colorado, hoping to find my niche in this unfamiliar town.

LIFE LESSONS FROM A BENCHWARMER

The transition to Colorado was a challenging chapter for me, especially as I navigated my freshman year at Harrison High School. Although I was eager to join the football team, I found myself on the sidelines, unable to break into the already-established roster. When basketball season rolled around, I was thrilled to make the final cut for the freshman team—a proud moment that was unfortunately overshadowed by limited playing time. I knew I had the talent, but without my dad there to advocate for me during practices and games, I felt like I was fighting an uphill battle.

I couldn't help but notice the contrast between my situation and that of another freshman whose father attended every practice. His relentless support eventually earned his son a spot on the city's top-ranked varsity team. While I wasn't overly concerned about being better than him—after all, I joined the basketball team primarily to avoid being home—I did see others who were clearly more skilled getting overlooked. Those frustrating moments taught me a lesson about advocacy and perseverance: While talent and skill are crucial, having someone in your corner can be the difference between sitting on the bench and seizing opportunities.

It became clear that advocating for myself was essential, whether through seeking guidance, standing up for my worth, or surrounding myself with people who believed in me. I learned that resilience isn't just about facing setbacks but also about mustering the courage to fight for what you deserve.

The social challenges of having no close friends, finding myself at the end of the bench, and lacking romantic prospects led me to turn to my studies for solace. I dedicated myself to my coursework and ended the year with perfect grades, a reassuring achievement during a difficult time.

While I didn't forge lifelong friendships at Harrison High, I did find camaraderie in the cafeteria, joining in on my teammates' conversations. I empathized with their complaints—"Can you believe they scheduled a test on Friday, just before our big game?" one buddy would grumble, and I'd nod along, sharing in their exaggerated frustrations, even though my academic success was the only bright spot in my life at that time.

Being a studious kid in a lower-income neighborhood often felt isolating, especially as I discovered the stigma around academic achievement in many minority communities. Many saw valuing education as a departure from the norm. In contrast, friends from more vibrant, academically focused backgrounds reveled in their academic successes, proudly integrating them into their sports accolades, like "academic all-conference honors." I hold onto the hope that one day, in all communities, academic achievement will be celebrated just as passionately as athletic prowess, allowing young people to embrace their intellectual curiosity without the pressure to conform.

GRATEFUL FOR THESE GUYS

After moving to Fort Carson, I found myself navigating my third high school out of five: Fountain Fort Carson High School. This school remains etched in my memory as it was the setting for some of my most cherished experiences. What set Fountain Fort Carson apart was its unwavering celebration of student-athletes, regardless of their backgrounds. The school boasted two legendary coaches, Mitch Johnson and Art Hassler, both of whom are honored in the Colorado High School Hall of Fame.

Here, I met two coaches who truly guided me: Coach Charles Paddock and Coach Mike "Mo" Maiurro. My previous experiences at Harrison High in both football and basketball had left me feeling disheartened, so I dedicated my summer to improving and turning things around for my sophomore year.

On the first day of football practice, as I lined up with the tight ends and caught a few passes, Coach Paddock rushed over and said, "Young man, go over there with the running backs. With those calves, we'll figure it out." And figure it out we did. In my junior year, I had a standout performance against Harrison High, the very school that had left me sitting on the end of the bench just eighteen months prior.

Then there was Coach Mo, who remains a good friend to this day. He made it clear he was putting me on the basketball team for three reasons: defense, culture, and grades. We both understood my role was to distribute assists and play defense rather than shoot the ball. At least I knew where

I stood, and both coaches served as fantastic mentors for countless young men and women.

My sophomore year at Fountain Fort Carson was fulfilling. By the time I became a junior, I had earned academic all-conference recognition and attracted interest from several colleges for football and basketball. I began exploring West Point, which would allow me to combine my passion for the military with academic rigor and the opportunity to play sports.

Two remarkable Fountain Fort Carson graduates from a couple years ahead of me reignited my drive to be well rounded: Ian Weikel and Dante Stewart. Ian embodied hard work and determination. Serving as the quarterback for the football team and the point guard for basketball, he was the quintessential "all-American" kid. His dedication on and off the field was truly inspiring. After high school, Ian attended West Point, which motivated me to aim for the same goal.

Dante Stewart, a local legend, was known for his achievements in football, basketball, and track and field. He excelled both athletically and academically, maintaining his status as an honors student while remaining grounded and well loved by all. His ability to balance success in sports with academic excellence while staying humble was genuinely inspiring.

Watching Ian and Dante in action reignited my sense of purpose. Their accomplishments reminded me of my potential and sparked my desire to fully embrace life. Before attending Fountain Fort Carson, I had solid grades, but the inspiration I drew from Ian Weikel and Dante Stewart pushed my motivation to new heights. I became fixated on achieving nothing less than an A, driven by the ambition of securing a spot at West Point. Additionally, my father's commitment to the military provided me with a unique advantage and further fueled my aspirations for the Academy.

I had the goal of making my coaches and all of Fountain Fort Carson High proud by sending another graduate to West Point. Everything seemed to be pointing that way. As senior year approached, a few new athletes moved to town, and it looked like we were going to be one of the top football teams in the state. I was ecstatic and ready to get my senior year started. Then, the worst news that could have hit me at the time arrived. My dad announced he had received new military orders sending us to Fort Polk, Louisiana. I could not believe my ears. I was on track to receive all-conference honors in football and possibly even make a run at the state title, and now, I had to move to Louisiana and hope to make the team. I was genuinely upset, feeling like a chapter of my life was abruptly closing before I had the chance to fully write it.

As I prepared for this unexpected transition, I reflected on all the lessons I had learned at Fountain Fort Carson. The resilience, dedication, and camaraderie I had built would stay with me even as I faced a new beginning. While the thought of leaving everything I had worked for behind was disheartening, I realized challenges could also be opportunities for growth. My new chapter awaited, and I was determined to carry the spirit of my coaches and teammates with me. As I stepped into the unknown, I held tightly to the belief that I could forge new paths and continue to strive for excellence no matter where I was. All I had was hope.

FROM STAR TO MID

The change of schools hit me hard this time, and I had no choice but to comply. As I entered my senior year, I was now headed to my fourth high school out of five. Going from being an all-conference player to facing the unknown of competing just to get on a team was a wild experience. Leaving behind the vibrant environment of Colorado Springs—known for its beautiful scenery and active social life—was tough. Fort Polk, Louisiana, felt like the polar opposite of Colorado Springs. It was anything but beautiful or vibrant, almost isolated. However, I did know one thing about Louisiana: all coaches respect the state for its athletic talent, especially in football. I needed to adapt quickly and make strategic decisions.

At that time, I had a car. It wasn't anything glamorous—just an old Dodge minivan that I bought with money I earned working at Popeye's Chicken back in Colorado Springs—but having a car allowed me some choice in which school I would attend.

Option one was Leesville High School—it was larger, with more social activities, and probably a more fun place to be. Option two was Pickering High School, which was smaller and located in a less dynamic community.

The decision seemed clear: I should attend Leesville High School. However, Leesville had one of the top athletes in high school sports running the ball at the time, Cecil Collins. He received the ball at least twenty-five times a game, averaging eight yards per carry. I didn't need a psychic to tell me that I would likely be riding the bench or blocking for him all year. If you watch his film at LSU, you'll understand.

Pickering also had a star running back, Robert Williams. The difference was that while Rob carried the ball only twenty times a game and Pickering ran a veer option, allowing other running backs to share those carries and get some film. Therefore, Pickering was the more logical choice if I wanted to keep my recruitment prospects alive.

I used the track season to settle in at Pickering. In Colorado, my fifty-two-second four-hundred-meter dash could have propelled me to at least the regionals. In Louisiana, though, I had a 0 percent chance of getting out of my own conference with that time. As for my 11.3 in the one-hundred-meter? Forget about it; I wasn't going to medal at a regular meet. So, I focused on the relay teams, where we were only a few seconds away from making it to the state finals in the four-by-four-hundred-meter relay. Tuxie Peoples, you ran a fantastic race that day, brother.

Track put me in prime shape for football at Pickering. My role on the team wasn't as prominent as it had been in Colorado, but I made the most of the opportunities I was presented and had some notable performances. Academically, I was on top of my game. I took most of my courses via video stream from the local college—this was like Skype two decades before Skype! I also made the academic all-conference team and found my way onto student government—not bad for a guy who showed up at the very end of junior year.

With six months left until high school graduation, I had made some good friends at Pickering. I was looking forward to receiving responses from colleges about where I would spend the next four years after high school. Life was good—until it suddenly wasn't.

My dad came to me with another announcement: He had orders to deploy to Haiti in support of "Operation Uphold Democracy." My stepmother, now with two young children, decided to move in with her parents during my dad's deployment. Since we could not stay in Louisiana, my younger brother and I moved in with my dad's mom, Zenobia Mitchell, also known as Grandma Z, in Cincinnati, Ohio. Now, I was attending my fifth high school!

The new school was named Mt. Healthy. Upon arriving in Cincinnati, I did two things: I joined the track team and got a job at McDonald's. I needed the job mainly to get out of Grandma Z's reach. However, my life took a turn when that McDonald's was robbed at gunpoint and the assailant pointed his gun directly at me as I handed him the cash from both registers. Most people would have panicked, but this was not the first time I had been robbed or even shot at. I decided not to tell Grandma Z about this incident because she was very strict and would definitely have made me quit my job.

Grandma Z was a disciplined woman who had been a teacher for over fifty years. Our relationship was tough; it often felt like I had wronged her in a previous life. However, when the high school administration accused me of being a gang member due to a photo I took with a track baton (they couldn't see the baton between my hands and mistakenly thought I was making a "C" sign for Crip), Grandma Z went to the school and confronted them.

When I graduated from Mt. Healthy, I wasn't invited to any graduation parties; I just sort of faded into the background. The unexpected shift to my fifth high school disrupted my preparations for the ACT. Although my academic record and football recruitment were strong, the abrupt move resulted in a solid ACT score instead of a great one.

Despite this, West Point admissions and the coaches presented me with an opportunity. Instead of gaining direct admission to West Point, I was accepted into the United States Military Academy Preparatory School (USMAPS). I now had options. As I closed the chapter on my high school career and prepared to head off to college, I reflected on the relentless and winding journey I navigated to get there.

CHAPTER 3 TRIGGERS

In Chapter 3, I reflected on pivotal moments that significantly impacted my mental well-being and laid the groundwork for future struggles. A tapestry of triggers emerged, intricately woven into the fabric of my journey. The echoes of the past resonate; each trigger is a brushstroke painting the emotional and psychological landscape of my life.

- The memory of being cast as Fat Albert in a school play at Fort Knox lingers. It planted the seeds of self-consciousness and body-image insecurities that would take root and grow within me.
- The injury I sustained during the Oklahoma drill in Germany stands out as a defining moment where physical pain intertwined with emotional turmoil. This left me yearning for validation through physical prowess while grappling with the weight of my shattered ankle.
- The departure of my brother Ronald to South Carolina marked a turning point, thrusting me into a role of responsibility. This sudden shift in family dynamics, coupled with my dad's new marriage, left me navigating the uncharted waters of pressure and loss.
- Each trigger—from biased teachers in eighth grade to confrontations—served as a mirror reflecting the harsh realities of judgment and vulnerability in both the adult and adolescent worlds.
- The transition from Fort Carson to Fort Polk brought additional challenges to my journey, underscoring the significance of advocacy and adaptability while navigating feelings of isolation and adversity.
- My father's deployment to Haiti resulted in an unexpected move to Cincinnati, abruptly interrupting my academic trajectory and hindering my preparations for the future.
- Facing false accusations of gang affiliation and being the victim of a robbery added layers of injustice that threatened my aspirations.

Throughout these tumultuous experiences, a persistent lack of recognition and validation at home acted as a constant undercurrent, fueling feelings of neglect and nurturing a craving for external approval. This craving would shape my self-image and mask the emotional toll within.

As I navigate these triggers, I am reminded of their profound impact on my mental health, paving the way for self-discovery, healing, and the resilience needed to forge ahead with newfound strength and clarity.

Part II

MAKING OF A SOLDIER

CHAPTER 4

WEST POINT

I WAS A BIT DISAPPOINTED WHEN WEST POINT DID NOT ACCEPT me directly. This news left me feeling down, but at the same time, I was excited about my other options. Given how I had juggled school, a full-time job, sports, and financial constraints throughout middle and high school, the outcome was, in retrospect, quite positive.

My options outside of West Point included several mid-major football scholarships and a full-ride Reserve Officers' Training Corps (ROTC) scholarship to my chosen historically Black college, Grambling State. When you're eighteen years old, an extra year of school, like for USMAPS, can seem like a long commitment. I was tempted to take the easy route and use my ROTC scholarship to attend Grambling State and walk onto the football team.

However, common sense kicked in when I realized Grambling would have many skilled players like me, and I wasn't particularly fond of Louisiana. I came to understand that taking an extra year to prepare academically would be beneficial. Therefore, I decided to bet on myself, turning down the other academic, athletic, and ROTC scholarships to commit to attending USMAPS. In the end, this proved to be the right decision.

A MOMENT OF CLARITY

Transitioning to USMAPS was transformative for me. The school's motto "Desire, Faith, Effort" embodies its mission to prepare candidates for academic and military success at West Point. The monthlong basic training was more mentally challenging than physically demanding, allowing me to embrace the focus and discipline I needed. As Cadet Candidate Ritter, my newfound sense of freedom and independence was truly liberating. My main concerns shifted to adhering to the rules and enhancing my academic aptitude for the upcoming ACT and SAT tests. For the first time in ages, I enjoyed a full eight hours of sleep each night, free from the burdens of fashion choices or financial worries. Despite my initial hesitation, I found my time at USMAPS to be incredibly enriching.

I consider myself fortunate to have attended USMAPS. The upheavals and constant changes in my life had deprived me of the resources needed to excel at standardized tests. The public schools I attended often lacked adequate resources and did not provide preparatory classes for admissions exams.

At Mount Healthy High School, the graduation rate for African American students was alarmingly low, and at Pickering High School, several students dropped out to work construction jobs, which derailed our football season. Consequently, the schools' priorities leaned toward helping students earn their diplomas rather than preparing them for elite institutions. Nonetheless, I achieved above-average scores on standardized tests, which opened crucial doors for my future. The most significant of these was the chance to prepare for my dream school in just one year.

I recognized that competing with students who had access to superior high school educations at West Point would require the specialized training offered at USMAPS. With determination, I set aside my doubts and committed to my goals. In today's competitive athletic landscape, many athletes attend prep schools or junior colleges to gain an edge and compete at the Division I level. However, my experience at USMAPS was primarily academic, not athletic. Upon graduating from high school, I was an above-average athlete and aware of my potential. While my football recruitment showed promise, there were thousands of other athletes at my position with equal or more talent. This underscored the reality that Division I athletes, regardless of school, are exceptional, and I found myself surrounded by peers who shared the same goal of graduating from West Point. Academics are the primary focus at West Point, a fact that was made glaringly clear at the prep school. Even at USMAPS, students were expelled for failing to meet grade requirements. USMAPS had one goal: prepare students for the academic rigors of West Point. Everything else was secondary.

At USMAPS, my sole mission was to secure my acceptance to West Point. There was no room for distractions or side paths. I was so dedicated to going to West Point and graduating with the West Point class of 2000 that I got "West Point Class of 2000" tattooed on my arm during my first semester at USMAPS. This tattoo solidified my objective, and that level of dedication is rare. My classmate Johnny Johnson still laughs at my tattoo three decades later. However, the tattoo put my path in writing and reminded me of my goal each day. I wasn't worried about what everyone else was doing; I knew exactly where I was headed, and I was locked in.

I believe this is what made prep school such a defining period for me. It allowed me to concentrate intently on my goal, free from all the noise. I was no longer simply hoping for success; I was right on the cusp of it, ready to do whatever it took to achieve it. I viewed this opportunity as a chance for generational change in my family. It was a rare moment when everything made sense, and I knew, without a doubt, that I was on the right path.

DESIRE, FAITH, AND EFFORT PAY OFF

USMAPS football team after beating Navy (#42, bottom left)

A lot of good men in this photo—USMAPS football team, 1995

I would be remiss if I did not discuss the location of USMAPS in 1995. The school was situated in New Jersey, about an hour-and-a-half drive from New York City. Initially, I didn't venture into the city much because I needed to focus on my academic performance. However, once I hit my academic stride, I gained more freedom.

Cadet candidates on the honor roll were allowed to take leave and head into the city. I had spent time in New York City as a kid at my grandmother's place in Harlem, but returning as a young adult was a completely different experience—it was nothing like the small towns and suburbs I was used to. The energy, noise, and hustle of the city felt alive. Walking around New York gave me a sense of independence and adventure that was starkly different from my routine at school or my upbringing.

My newfound freedom and privileges at USMAPS were undoubtedly exciting. However, the best part of USMAPS was the friendships I built while there, which made the year unforgettable. I met some of my closest friends at USMAPS, people I still keep in touch with today. There's something about being in an environment where everyone is striving for the same goal that fosters strong bonds. We studied, trained, and encouraged each other to improve while also enjoying time off together and embarking on random adventures. For many of us, this was our first time away from home, and we relied on each other to stay on track, ensuring that we all graduated and matriculated to West Point. The excitement was palpable as we envisioned ourselves walking through the gates of West Point, our hearts burning with a hunger to succeed. This feeling lasted throughout the year as we awaited our acceptances. Being surrounded by like-minded individuals who understood the sacrifices and dedication required to achieve our common goal was a powerful motivator. Skin color, gender, and ethnicity didn't matter; everyone was recognized as a vital part of the community. Of course, we did have a few bad seeds who tried to climb over others, but for the most part, cooperation thrived. Looking back, those friendships were the most significant outcome of my USMAPS experience. We were all in the same boat, working toward a common goal, creating a bond difficult to describe.

My year at USMAPS flew by, and soon the standardized test dates for

West Point approached. Going into the SAT, I felt much more confident this time. I felt like I had the wind at my back, propelling me into the test. Armed with the right resources, I dedicated myself to studying, tackling every practice test, and honing my skills. USMAPS's resources and structured environment provided a significant boost, and I made the most of it, feeling primed to conquer the test that stood between me and my dream.

As I sat down to take the SAT, my heart pounded like a drum, its rhythmic beat echoing in my ears. My palms grew damp with anticipation, and my mind raced with the endless possibilities of what could go wrong. Yet, I took a deep breath, steadied my nerves, and began. With each question, my focus sharpened and my determination intensified. I approached each problem with precision, my pencil moving with purpose.

The wait for the test results was long, and I grew restless. When they finally arrived, I was elated. I had performed exceptionally well on the SAT. All those hours of studying, the sacrifices I had made, and the gamble I had taken on myself led to this moment of happiness. Then came the day I received my official acceptance letter to West Point. The feeling was indescribable—a mix of joy, pride, and disbelief. I remember sitting there with the admissions letter in my hand, reading the words repeatedly, trying to grasp what it meant. It felt like a weight had been lifted off my shoulders. All the challenges, doubts, and obstacles I had faced were worth it, and finally, a major goal had been achieved.

No one in the world was happier than I was that day. I could finally see the culmination of all my efforts and sacrifices. It was a victory not just for me but for everyone who had supported me along the way. Overwhelmed with a profound sense of satisfaction and confidence, I felt as if a new path was unfolding before me. I knew West Point would present its challenges, but I was prepared. The journey to get there had shaped me, and I felt ready to take on whatever lay ahead.

DUTY, HONOR, COUNTRY

First day at West Point marching with my Beast Squad

Excited and filled with anticipation, I arrived at West Point. My first day was nothing short of chaotic, a whirlwind of new rules and intense expectations. As I drove through the front gate, I couldn't help but think about the esteemed graduates I was joining, including General Douglas MacArthur and General Dwight D. Eisenhower. MacArthur famously said in an address to the cadets at West Point in 1962, "Duty, honor, country: Those three hallowed words reverently dictate what you ought to be, what you can be, what you will be."

As soon as I stepped onto the grounds and reported to the cadet with the red sash, it was clear everything was different from what I had known. They drilled into us that there were only three acceptable responses at West Point: "Yes, sir," "No, sir," or "Sir, I don't understand." It felt like an entirely new language I was being completely immersed in.

The first day was packed with a barrage of instructions and rules designed to get us oriented and ready for the rigorous road ahead, which included a decent amount of hazing and some physical training. One hour into onboarding, we were told we needed to prepare for a parade, which sounded exciting but daunting. I thought, *Who does a parade on day one? That's right, welcome to West Point.* It was a spectacle of precision and discipline, and West Point wanted to show parents and supporters of the new recruits just how quickly the Academy impacts cadets.

The first time we tried to fall into formation for this parade, a tiny, fierce woman in uniform barked instructions at us. Her voice cut through the air with sharp authority. She seemed to have an endless reserve of energy, and her demands were relentless. Her yelling was intense, making it hard not to feel overwhelmed.

The whole experience was a culture shock. Never before had I felt so much fear of a small, Caucasian woman! The structure, discipline, and sheer intensity of it all were a far cry from the relatively relaxed atmosphere I was used to. But amid the confusion and pressure, there was a strange sense of exhilaration. I felt like I was on the brink of something significant that would push me far beyond my previous limits. Here I was, part of something deeply rooted in American history—a tradition that had shaped the nation. The history and prestige of West Point were palpable, and being granted access to this storied institution was an honor. The sweat and frustration of the day were worth it knowing I had earned my place in West Point Class of 2000.

Even though the first day was tough and the learning curve steep, I felt a surge of pride and gratitude for the opportunity. Despite the chaos that marked my very unconventional first day, I slept peacefully that night, waiting for the sun to rise and bring more chaos in all its glory. However, even the enthusiastic side of me knew that the transition from prep school to West Point would be a challenging one. At USMAPS, the environment was structured and disciplined, overseen by career officers and top-notch noncommissioned officers. These supervisors were experienced professionals who guided us with a blend of authority and mentorship, always maintaining high professionalism. They focused on preparing us physically and emotionally to ensure we were ready for West Point. While they were strict, the overall environment was supportive.

West Point, however, operated on a completely different level. Upperclassmen ran the Corps, and the hierarchy was rigid and uncompromising. Regardless of size or background, every new cadet was at the mercy of every upperclassman. The first few months at West Point centered on humbling new cadets, and I certainly felt that impact.

To navigate the challenges of this demanding environment, I quickly learned not to take things personally. It was essential to maintain a level of detachment and understand that being treated harshly was part of the process. The goal was to first break you down before building you back up. The first year was all about that breakdown. I focused on following orders to the best of my ability, which was crucial to avoiding additional criticism and trouble. Following the rules and meeting expectations became my survival strategy, and I had always been a survivor.

COLONEL THAYER'S METHOD

One of my unconventional strategies for navigating my first year at West Point was to prioritize sleep. Given the strict schedule and constant demands of cadet life, I realized managing stress effectively required being well rested. By maximizing my sleep, I found it easier to handle challenges, allowing me to face each new task with renewed energy.

At West Point, cadets had to excel in three key areas: academics, physical training, and military training. Success in all three disciplines was required for graduation. While each area demanded significant effort and dedication, the academic challenges were particularly daunting. I often found myself studying late into the night by flashlight, the quiet sounds of pages turning and notes being scribbled serving as the backdrop to my prep sessions for upcoming tests and frequent pop quizzes.

The Thayer Method of learning presented my biggest academic challenge. This approach required cadets to read and understand the assigned material before attending class. Professors often tested us on content that had not yet been discussed, expecting us to be prepared regardless. This was a stark departure from my previous educational experiences and emphasized active learning, practice, and immediate feedback. Unfortunately, in those early months, that feedback often resulted in painfully low scores.

Embracing the Thayer Method pushed me to engage deeply with the material and be ready to apply what I had learned in real time. It became clear that simple comprehension was not sufficient; I needed to come prepared to discuss and apply the concepts. Looking back, I see how this method prepares cadets for future professional challenges. While the Thayer Method made learning more demanding, it also made it more effective. Each day brought new challenges, accompanied by the ever-present pressure to perform well.

The most intense experiences of my plebe year occurred during that first academic semester. Coming from the background of attending five different public high schools, I found the high level and rapid pace of West Point academics to be incredibly challenging.

One particularly memorable assignment came from my math class, which focused on discrete dynamical systems. My partners and I were tasked with analyzing various mathematical equations, developing alternative solutions, and presenting our findings. We faced a steep learning curve and little guidance from the professor, who employed the Thayer Method.

None of us in my group knew how to tackle this assignment. We didn't know each other, so we all assumed someone else would take the lead—this didn't happen until one partner, Joseph Jones, sent an email the day before the deadline. With only hours left, we hastily assembled one of the worst Excel models ever built.

After shaking hands and hoping to simply not fail, we were relieved when we ultimately received a D-plus. After my first semester, my GPA stood at 2.3; while I wasn't thriving, I was at least surviving.

As I entered my second semester, I realized I needed a more effective approach if I wanted to succeed academically. I reached out to my good friends Anthony Thompson and Daryl Ferguson, and together, we formed a study group.

Meeting in the library at least twice a week, we soon discovered where each of us was strongest. Daryl emerged as our math expert—a crucial asset considering West Point's focus on engineering. This collective effort improved our understanding of the material and fostered a sense of camaraderie that made the demanding environment feel more manageable.

Through this experience, I learned the importance of seeking support and collaborating with others to navigate the challenges at West Point. This approach enabled me to graduate with a GPA of over 3.0, which is a notable achievement at West Point.

THE WEST POINT WAY

At West Point, physical fitness was considered as important as intellectual fitness. While not every cadet had the physique of a statue of some Greek god, many did. The standards for physical fitness were high, and meeting those standards was essential for both performance and overall readiness. Cadets were required to pass a physical fitness test every quarter, which assessed running, push-ups, sit-ups, and completion of a cadet obstacle course.

Maintaining top physical shape was both encouraged and required. Physical training sessions were a consistent part of our schedules, and we were required to maintain a healthy body weight while demonstrating proficiency in essential exercises. West Point followed a unique philosophy: "Every cadet is an athlete." Even if you were not competing in college athletics, you were expected to participate in several intramural sports to keep your fitness grade up and foster camaraderie with fellow cadets.

As part of our fitness coursework, all male cadets were required to complete classes in boxing, swimming, and gymnastics. While it was a significant workload, it was essential for preparing us for the challenges we would face in the future. There were two gym courses that every freshman had to pass to graduate: swimming and boxing.

The swimming class at West Point was actually quite amusing. All the lowest-ranked swimmers were placed in the same class, humorously dubbed "rock swimming" because we all seemed destined to sink like a rock to the bottom of the pool as soon as we entered the water. For their part, the instructors would stand at the side of the pool and watch us sink only to fish us out with a rod before we drowned.

When you first walked into the rock-swimming class, you might think you walked in on a photo shoot with a group of African American fitness models. The class was filled with impressively sculpted students, including running backs, wide receivers, and defensive backs from the football team and a substantial number of basketball players. It resembled a feature in the African American section of *Men's Health* magazine—until we were told to get into the water, at which point our appearance of athletic prowess was betrayed by us dropping straight to the bottom of the pool.

The group of rock swimmers I was in was historically bad; we were so inept we were ordered to swim twice a day: once at 6:00 a.m. and again during our scheduled swim class. I must give credit to the Academy, though, by the end of the semester, everyone in that class could swim competently and maintain enough composure in the water to use our pants as flotation devices. The final test involved swimming laps for ninety minutes, and we all passed with flying colors, no longer rock swimmers.

Most of our rock-swimming class eventually transitioned to boxing, where we were joined by our Caucasian teammates who had been in the more advanced swim class. Our boxing class consisted of athletes weighing between 180 and 225 pounds. The boxing course was typically the most intense at West Point, especially if you were not a Division I athlete and placed in the class based solely on your weight. This often resulted in clashes between two hundred pounds of muscle and two hundred pounds of baby fat, leading to predictably harsh outcomes. It was West Point's cold, hard way of advising a cadet to work off the baby fat, much like how West Point required African American football players to learn to swim—a harsh and stark reality.

One of the most challenging aspects of the physical training program at West Point was the Indoor Obstacle Training Course. This facility was designed to test and enhance our physical fitness, agility, and problem-solving. The course included a variety of obstacles, such as walls, ropes, monkey bars, balance beams, and climbing structures, each simulating real-world challenges we might face in military operations. Successfully navigating the course required speed, agility, endurance, and determination. The indoor environment allowed us to train year-round regardless of weather conditions, ensuring we could always improve our physical readiness. I approached these physical challenges with the same dedication I applied to my studies.

As I settled into life at West Point, I began to develop the third pillar of my training: military skills and leadership. This component brought together everything I had learned about academics and physical fitness and synthesized them into real-world scenarios. Quick and precise decision-making is essential as a combat arms officer, and West Point prepared me to employ it even in the most challenging environments. My first field training exercise at West Point felt like stepping into a different world. We were placed in a simulated combat situation, where every choice mattered. I remember that day well. It was cold and raining, and I ate my breakfast of wet, cold eggs with wet toast from my wet bunker. With the sounds of mock gunfire and urgent commands of the platoon sergeant echoing around us, I had to rely on my practiced skills and quick thinking.

At this point, I was just a member of a squad with seven of my peers. I only needed to get myself through this high-pressure environment, where I found even leading and motivating myself to be a challenge. These simulations created a building block that would eventually allow me to manage myself and lead others in real-world combat situations, even if during the drill, all I could think about was warm breakfast and a bed.

Leadership development was rolled into military training at West Point. As cadets advanced through their four years, they were challenged with progressively larger leadership opportunities within the Corps of Cadets, going from leading small groups to managing larger teams. Each leadership role came with its own challenges, and cadets were evaluated on how well they led, made decisions, and maintained overall military discipline.

PRIORITIZING HEALTH

One additional challenge I faced at West Point was starting my cadet career as a member of the college football team. To clarify, "playing" for the team didn't mean I made it onto television; it meant I successfully made the team, which was a significant accomplishment given that most West Point running backs ranged in height from five eight to five ten, weighed between 185 and 220 pounds, and often ran a 4.6-second forty-yard dash. The Academy essentially recruited the same person over and over again, and you had to significantly differentiate yourself to earn playing time. I always seemed to mess up something in practice, such as a blocking assignment. At West Point, if you mess up a blocking assignment, you will never play again. Despite my limited chance of playing, being part of the team added another layer of pride, camaraderie, responsibility, and commitment to my cadet experience.

However, something unexpected happened that tested my resolve. After several football practices my sophomore year, I began experiencing intense and debilitating migraine headaches. These migraines made it hard for me to focus and perform academically and on the football field.

Initially, I tried to push through the pain, thinking it was just a minor issue that would pass. But the headaches persisted and grew worse. I was hesitant to seek medical treatment because I knew if I was deemed unfit to serve as an army officer, West Point would send me home—period, no exceptions. I had witnessed great athletes being medically dismissed from the Academy due to injuries. The thought of facing a similar fate was terrifying. My legacy depended on graduating from West Point, and nothing was going to stop me from achieving that dream. I was determined that a West Point degree would not slip away due to a medical issue.

Additionally, my mother had endured a brain tumor that almost killed her my freshman year, a few months prior to the start of my own head issues. Her health battle weighed heavily on my mind and complicated my situation. I felt a deep sense of responsibility not just to my goals but also to my family, knowing firsthand how health issues can derail a life.

My migraine condition forced me to make the most difficult decision I had faced to that point. I had to weigh my commitment to football against my long-term ambition of graduating from West Point. I realized that continuing to play football while dealing with these severe headaches could jeopardize my overall well-being and academic achievement. It wasn't just about the physical pain; it was about maintaining my performance in all areas of my West Point training.

After much consideration, I decided to step away from football. Although it was a difficult choice after investing so much time and effort into the sport, I knew my health and my studies were more critical to my long-term success than football. In hindsight, this was a wise decision for my future, but at the time, it was an extremely tough one.

I needed to focus on completing my training and achieving my West Point degree, no matter the cost. Quitting football was a significant sacrifice, and it was the first time in my life I ever quit anything, but it was the right choice.

Quitting football allowed me to manage my headaches better and succeed in my academic and military training at West Point. I received a lot of criticism from former teammates, and I understood their frustration. I couldn't go around disclosing my condition, as that might jeopardize my graduation, so I embraced the challenge with a clear sense of purpose and determination, reminding myself that my goal was to earn a West Point degree, get into the military, and deal with everything else as it came.

One stark reality about West Point that anyone entering must understand is this: In the late 1990s, West Point admitted around twelve hundred new cadets annually, but only eight hundred graduated on average. I reminded myself of this fact every time I questioned my resolve.

CHAPTER 4 TRIGGERS

Reflecting on my time at West Point, several moments stand out as triggers that shaped my mental health and may have contributed to future challenges. These instances were pivotal, not just in my journey to becoming a soldier but also in how they impacted my emotional resilience and mental well-being.

- The disappointment of not being accepted directly into West Point—that news hit me hard—left me feeling inadequate despite my achievements. I had worked tirelessly, juggling school, a full-time job, sports, and financial constraints, yet I had fallen short. This moment planted seeds of self-doubt, making me question whether I was truly capable of achieving my dreams. While I eventually saw USMAPS as a positive experience, the initial sting of rejection lingered.

- At USMAPS, the intense focus on academics and standardized testing was another trigger. Coming from schools with limited resources, I felt the weight of competing against peers who had far superior educational backgrounds. The pressure to excel academically while preparing for the ACT and SAT was overwhelming. I knew that failure meant losing my chance at West Point, and this constant fear of falling short created a mental strain I carried with me.
- Arriving at West Point was a culture shock that triggered feelings of fear and inadequacy. The rigid hierarchy, relentless hazing, and sheer intensity of the environment were unlike anything I had experienced before. The first day, with its chaotic onboarding and fierce commands from the tiny woman in uniform, left me feeling overwhelmed and out of place. The transition from the supportive structure of USMAPS to the unforgiving atmosphere of West Point was jarring, and I struggled to adapt to the constant scrutiny and high expectations.
- The most significant trigger from this period was the onset of debilitating migraines during football practices. These headaches were not just physically painful; they were mentally draining, making it difficult to focus on academics and training. The fear of being medically dismissed from West Point added another layer of anxiety. I felt trapped, unable to disclose my condition fully, knowing it could jeopardize my future. This internal conflict—between prioritizing my health and achieving my goals—was emotionally taxing and left me feeling isolated.
- The emotional toll of my mother's health battle with a brain tumor during my freshman year was tremendous. Her near-death experience weighed heavily on me, amplifying my stress and sense of responsibility. I felt the pressure to succeed not just for myself but for my family, knowing how fragile life can be. This compounded my mental strain as I tried to balance my challenges with the weight of my family's struggles.
- The decision to quit football resulted in feelings of loss and guilt. Football had been a significant part of my identity, and walking away felt like abandoning a piece of myself. The criticism from former team-

mates only deepened my sense of isolation, especially since I couldn't fully explain my reasons without risking my degree. This decision, while necessary, left me grappling with feelings of failure and a fear of judgment.

These triggers—disappointment, pressure, cultural shock, health struggles, family crises, and sacrifice—shaped my mental health during this chapter of my life. They taught me resilience but also left scars I carried forward.

Looking back, I see how these moments contributed to my future challenges, forcing me to confront my limits while striving to achieve my goals.

CHAPTER 5

FORWARD, MARCH!

FROM A YOUNG AGE, I VIEWED WEST POINT AS AN INSTITUTION of higher learning with the added benefit of training young people to become leaders of character for the military and beyond. West Point is known for its honor code, which states, "A cadet may not lie, cheat, steal, or tolerate those who do."

The school boasts graduates from diverse backgrounds and ethnicities who, even if they do not pursue a career in the military, commit to a lifetime of selfless service to the United States. A great example of this is Coach Michael Krzyzewski. If you think about the positive young people who grew into positive adults at West Point, you can visualize what it demands of its graduates. One of the most significant missions of West Point is to encourage young people to become better, more disciplined versions of themselves. This revelation came slowly as I moved through the Academy, and the dream of one day being among its ranks took on a deeper, more personal meaning for me.

The institution itself sits in a picturesque area on the Hudson River and gives the impression of a large, gray castle overlooking the river. The gray granite walls surrounding West Point felt like a giant, protective fortress that locked us cadets in and shielded us from negative elements that might hinder our performance and progress. However, they did not shield us from the institution's daily demands.

Life at the Academy was tough. From the outside, people see the prestige and honor of being a cadet but rarely understand the grind that defines each day. Unlike regular college students, who might enjoy some flexibility, sleep in after a late night at a fraternity party, or decide to skip a class here and there, our lives were ruled by the clock. Every minute was accounted for from dawn until lights out. It seemed as if a clock were ticking on our heads, even when we were asleep.

To this day, I strive to maximize each day to increase my productivity. However, I must watch myself or I can become involved in too many things, resulting in a lack of sleep and constantly pushing myself to do everything well and be all things to all people. I am a firm believer that multitasking and maintaining balance are keys to a successful life, and I am finally starting to heed my own advice.

At West Point, the classes, physical training, inspections, and endless responsibilities filled our days. Friday nights and weekends were when I completed the bulk of my work and took time to relax and mentally catch up.

I remember many weeknights spent studying by the light of a flashlight, long before cell phones existed. After lights out, when everything was supposed to be quiet, I would pull out a small flashlight and hide under my blanket to study without getting caught. This was the only time of day when I had complete liberty to study and figure things out on my own.

The soft light from my flashlight would barely illuminate the pages, but it was enough to keep me going. I didn't have a choice: There was always more to learn and memorize and not enough time during the day to do it all. Lying there in the dark, I would focus on my notes or textbooks, trying to finish just one more chapter or memorize a few more facts before the next morning.

My two roommates made fun of me when they discovered I was sacrificing sleep to improve my academic ranking, but that 2.3 GPA left me feeling insecure about potentially failing out of the Academy. Both of them just wanted to pass and move on, and one did not make it to their second year due to academic issues. I would find opportune times to rest during the day in between classes, whether it was inside my closet, under my bed, or propped up at my desk as if I were studying. I had one goal: survive.

THE LONGEST TABLE IN THE WORLD

As a freshman at West Point in the nineties, life was very different from any normal college experience. To begin with, we were rarely allowed to leave campus. Weekends off? Forget about it. Most of our time was spent on campus, either attending classes, training, or handling various duties. We were at the bottom of the food chain, and that meant we had a lot of extra responsibilities.

When we did start to get time off on weekends, we were typically trapped on campus with little to no entertainment. As such, this became the perfect time for me to reinvigorate my rap career, and my buddies and I formed a rap group to entertain ourselves and our classmates. And to have rap beefs with opposing rap groups. My buddy Cedric Bray was our producer, and our music initially sounded shaky. However, halfway through our freshman year, Ced finally found the right formula to refine the production. In fact, we got so popular that a significant number of our classmates would be waiting for us to send out a new song each Saturday via our class distribution email list. These songs were definitely explicit, and as I think back, West Point was probably not the place for this. However, it helped me interact with classmates I may have never met. It also kept us out of trouble as we were not idle. The group went on until we were juniors, and we even entered a few talent shows, placing decently high in the rankings.

One of the worst duties at West Point for a plebe was delivering laundry to the upperclassmen. You could be stuck at an upperclassman's door for five to ten minutes spouting off random West Point facts or what was reported in the *New York Times* that day before you were released to go back to the delivery room. Any issue with laundry was viewed as the fault of plebes. For example, if a T-shirt was missing, through no fault of your own, the taunting would go something like, "Plebe! My laundry's missing a T-shirt!" This would lead to you and several of your classmates running around unsuccessfully looking for the random T-shirt that was definitely lost by the cleaning service.

Another duty we had was serving at the breakfast and lunch tables. This meant keeping the glasses of the upperclassmen filled and performing other food-service tasks as requested. Some upperclassmen relished requesting random things, like 2.5 cubes of ice. Some plebes even carried a pie cutting template in case the upperclassmen decided they wanted a pie cut into seven equal slices. I never had a template; I would just mess the pie up and get yelled at!

Here is what you should know about the family-style dinner tables at West Point: They are the longest tables in the world. They are the only ones where it takes four years to move from the back of the table to the front.

REFLECTIONS FROM THE JOURNEY

At West Point in the 1990s, many rules made it nearly impossible for plebes (freshmen) to maintain relationships with those outside the Academy, including significant others. Those who entered West Point with an outside significant other and managed to stay with that person all the way to graduation became part of what we called the "2 Percent Club," although I believe the actual figure was closer to 0.5 percent.

Back in 1996, cell phones were not yet widespread, making it a chore to stay in touch with family, friends, or significant others. Pay phones were inconveniently located mostly in the basements of buildings, making it a brave endeavor for anyone to navigate the hallways to reach them. I was fortunate enough to avoid these issues.

The Academy's remote location also posed problems. West Point is situated in a secluded area, making it difficult to leave campus. Freshmen rarely earned the privilege of being allowed to leave, and even when they did later in their plebe year, they were required to wear their cadet uniforms and return by midnight.

There are many accomplishments I'm proud of from my time at West Point, but at the top of the list is simply graduating. For any cadet, graduation is a monumental achievement. The Academy is rigorous in every way—mentally, physically, and emotionally. There were days I doubted my ability to keep up with the relentless pace. However, standing there on graduation day, knowing I had overcome all the challenges, was a feeling I'll never forget. The long nights spent studying, early-morning trainings, and constant pressure to meet high standards all became worth it when I walked across that stage.

What made graduation even more special was that I graduated with a gold wreath on my uniform, an award given to cadets who ranked in the top 15 percent of their class in academics, military performance, and physical fitness. I hadn't planned for or expected this, but I pushed myself each year, striving not just to get by but to excel.

Another moment I'm proud of is being elected class vice president. Coming into West Point, I never could have imagined any of my classmates would vote for me, let alone elect me as a class leader. I would be remiss if I did not credit my rap hobby with helping me gain some votes—the saying "Any publicity is good publicity" definitely rang true in this situation. I had solid name recognition among my classmates as I entertained or perhaps offended them every weekend for our first two years together.

There is no greater honor than being chosen by esteemed peers for a leadership role. I took this honor seriously and worked hard to represent my class and collaborate with others to address concerns and plan events that made our time at West Point more enjoyable. I continue to do this more than two decades later for class reunions.

Finally, choosing Armor as my branch of service in the army was one of the best decisions I ever made. It wasn't an easy choice, but I knew I wanted to lead frontline combat soldiers and be involved in something both physically and mentally challenging. I wanted to be where the action was and lead soldiers through difficult situations. Armor felt like the right fit for me, combining leadership with hands-on tactical work. This decision ultimately shaped my military career, and I know I made the right choice.

MAJOR JOHN ROSEBOROUGH'S LEGACY

My fraternity brothers and me hanging out at Penn Relays in 2000

My fraternity brothers and me posing at West Point's Trophy Point in 2000

If I am asked about a major accomplishment that has shaped me into the person I am today outside of West Point, I can quickly and unequivocally answer that it was being part of a fraternity that has created many leaders and visionaries over the years. Becoming a charter member of the Alpha Phi Alpha Fraternity at West Point is a crown jewel among my achievements.

I was introduced to the fraternity very early on in my life. Alpha Phi Alpha Fraternity, Inc., was the first intercollegiate African American–founded Greek-letter fraternity, launched on December 4, 1906, at Cornell University by seven visionaries known as the "Seven Jewels." The fraternity has a long history of promoting leadership, scholarship, brotherhood, and service while also fighting for civil rights and social justice. The goals of the fraternity fit well with the goals of West Point and what it means to be a good human being.

Many of its members have played key roles in the advancement of the United States on a macro level and African Americans at the micro level. Dr. Martin Luther King Jr., Thurgood Marshall, Andrew Young, and Adam Clayton Powell Jr. are highly regarded members of my beloved fraternity.

I was honored to be a charter member of this fraternity, and it enabled me to connect with fraternity members at other universities in the Northeast and build additional bonds through networking. I love West Point, but the fraternity provided me a pathway to form a community outside its walls. The friendships I formed outside of West Point have been extremely valuable to me.

I don't want to do the fraternity a disservice by giving away too many of its secrets. However, please note that over one hundred men have benefited from being members of the West Point chapter of Alpha Phi Alpha over the past thirty years. I would be remiss if I did not pay homage to Major John Roseborough, may he rest in heaven, for mentoring hundreds of cadets as a tactical officer at West Point while also taking the time to connect and guide fellow Alpha Phi Alpha brothers. Major Roseborough was the ideal mentor. He was a beloved family man and the perfect blend of soldier and scholar with significant presence.

Major Roseborough was not a stout figure. However, the man did not need size; you could see the discipline on his face, and people respected him. An Armor officer, his uniform was always stiffly creased, and he wore the shiniest tanker boots I have ever seen. When my friends and I found out Major Roseborough was also an Alpha, we quickly set up a time to get his perspective on everything from being a combat arms officer to his views on family life to being a member of Alpha Phi Alpha and what it meant to him.

Major Roseborough took an interest in us and supported us every step of the way, helping us become men of Alpha Phi Alpha. More than anything, he stressed that we had a duty to give our best in academics, physical fitness, and military leadership to live up to the high standards that come with joining Alpha Phi Alpha and being a graduate of West Point.

Looking back, it's incredible to see how far our small chapter has come over almost thirty years. We boast fraternity alumni who have risen to the very senior levels of the military, as well as in professions such as medicine, law, venture capital, politics, education, and more. Many have earned advanced degrees from prestigious schools like Harvard, Duke, Columbia, Stanford, Wharton, Northwestern, and the University of Chicago. I could write an entire book about our chapter, but the point I want to make here is that through the mentorship of Brother John Roseborough, we started something special that has enabled us to lift each other up in our darkest hours and serve our communities. I know for a fact that if not for these men, I would not be here today.

As I reflect on my journey and the profound impact Major John Roseborough had on my life and the lives of so many others, I am filled with gratitude. His unwavering commitment to mentoring young men, dedication to excellence, and passion for fostering leadership have laid a strong foundation for our fraternity and the countless lives we've touched. Thank you, Major Roseborough, for believing in us, guiding us, and exemplifying what it means to be a true leader. Your legacy lives on in the bonds we share and positive contributions we strive to make in our communities. We are forever grateful for your influence and the indelible mark you left on our hearts and minds.

CHAPTER 5 TRIGGERS

Several circumstances that significantly impacted my mental health emerged during this time and are likely to have contributed to issues I grappled with later in life.

- From the outset, my perception of West Point as an esteemed institution filled with honor and integrity masked the intense pressures that lay beneath its surface. I remember the daunting realization of how tightly controlled our lives were, as each minute was dictated by a relentless schedule, leaving little room for flexibility or downtime. This rigid environment contributed to a constant sense of anxiety and urgency in me, which I can still feel today.
- One of the most impactful struggles for me during this time was maintaining my academic standing. I vividly recall the nights spent under my blanket with a flickering flashlight, frantically studying while my roommates snored beside me. This situation was more than just inconvenient; it was a significant source of stress that reflected my insecurities about my academic performance. That 2.3 GPA felt like balancing on the edge of a knife. I was haunted by the fear of failure, especially knowing that one of my peers had not made it to the second year due to similar issues. This comparison only heightened my anxiety, amplifying a persistent feeling of inadequacy that I carried with me long after my time at West Point.
- My relentless drive to excel, coupled with limited opportunities for rest, pushed me into a cycle of overexertion. I vividly remember finding random moments to catch a few winks—whether it was curled up in my closet or hunched over my desk pretending to study. Each of these experiences showcased my overwhelming desire to survive and succeed, yet they also initiated unhealthy coping mechanisms. I began to lose sight of balance, mistaking busyness for productivity, a pattern that would follow me into my adult life and lead to burnout.
- Living with roommates who had a more relaxed approach toward academics made me feel isolated in my pursuit of excellence. Their mockery of my late-night study habits compounded the pressure I

felt to prove myself. Instead of fostering camaraderie, these moments bred insecurity and loneliness. There were so many instances when I wished for a supportive environment, yet I felt I had to keep pushing myself to meet unrealistic expectations.

Ultimately, this chapter underscores the cumulative impact of pressure and isolation on my mental well-being. The brilliance of West Point's mission to cultivate leadership and character was often overshadowed by a culture that glorified overwork and a harsh competitive spirit.

However, amid the challenges, there were pockets of light that I cherished. The camaraderie developed within our class provided moments of relief and joy. The bond we formed during grueling training sessions and shared experiences fostered a sense of belonging that helped mitigate some of the stress. I recall the laughter and kind words exchanged during those rare moments of downtime, where it felt like we were all in it together. This fraternity forged through common hardships played a vital role in my overall resilience.

Additionally, I had the great fortune of having mentors like Major Roseborough, who became a guiding force during my time at the Academy. His encouragement and belief in my potential often reminded me that I was more than just a GPA; I was part of something greater. His presence offered a sense of stability amid the chaos, reinforcing the notion that while the pressures were real, I was equipped to manage them with the right support.

While I found strength in the bonds of brotherhood and mentorship, the challenges I faced during this developmental period acted as significant triggers for future mental-health struggles. They taught me that the pursuit of excellence, without balance and support, can lead to overwhelming anxiety and a fractured sense of self-worth.

CHAPTER 6

THE POWER OF RELATIONSHIPS

West Point class of 2000 class crest: "With Honor in Hand Two Thousand"

West Point senior photo—excited to move on

My time at West Point was about more than just military drills and classes; it was a transformative experience that taught me discipline, resilience, and how to lead others under pressure. Every day presented a new challenge, whether it involved meeting high physical standards, excelling in the classroom, or navigating the complexities of military life. By the time I graduated, I felt prepared to serve as a soldier and tackle any challenge the world might throw at me.

The early mornings, long nights, and relentless pace at West Point pushed me to become stronger and sharper. I learned to manage my time effectively, collaborate with others, and, most importantly, persevere when faced with difficulties. I developed a sense of responsibility and pride that I hadn't known before. It would not be an exaggeration to say I grew significantly during this time.

Walking across the stage on graduation day in my uniform, I felt a deep sense of accomplishment. I was prepared to enter the real world as a soldier, fully equipped with the skills and confidence necessary to thrive. I felt happy, proud, and purposeful, ready to take on whatever came next. As the ceremony—and my West Point journey—came to a close, I could sense my heartbeat quickening.

I had dreamed of this moment for a long time. I was now mentally, physically, and spiritually fit to lead the sons and daughters of America, and this moment validated all that preparation. My heart raced at this thought, and my smile grew wider. As I sat and waited for my turn to be handed my diploma, I could see the pride on the faces of my classmates. We were the West Point class of 2000. Our motto: "With honor in hand."

The night before graduation, I spent time with my roommate and fraternity brother T. J. Pope. We were buzzing with pride, excitement, and a touch of disbelief that this chapter of our lives was coming to an end. The reality that we were about to step into a new life—the life we had been preparing for—finally began to sink in.

I looked at T. J. and said, "I can't believe we made it, bro." My voice trailed off. "We're going out into the real world soon." He looked at me and nodded, a thoughtful expression on his face. "Same here. It's hard to believe we finally made it." We shared a firm handshake and a hug, anxiously awaiting the sunrise and tomorrow's graduation ceremony.

We sat together for a few minutes, reminiscing about our days at the Academy. We talked about the early mornings, harsh physical training, nights spent studying by flashlight, and friendships we built along the way. We also reflected on the road trips we took together to other universities to get a taste of college life.

There was something comforting about sitting there with T. J., knowing we shared the same challenges and triumphs. The sense of companionship was strong that night, and although we knew we would soon be going our separate ways to pursue our individual dreams, there was a quiet understanding that the bonds we had formed would keep us connected.

The immediate next step for 99 percent of West Point graduates following graduation was to enter military service. On our very first day at West Point, we had been told about the day we would officially become soldiers, and on the first day of our junior year, we had formally committed to serve this great nation as officers in its military. Joining the officer ranks was what we had spent years preparing for, and now, we were about to take everything we had learned over those four years into the real world.

After the graduation ceremonies and celebrations, reality hit: We were no longer cadets; we were no longer focused on simulated combat missions or assignments. We now had to lead actual soldiers and follow the orders of the commander in chief to address real-world problems, fight in literal wars, and carry out dangerous tasks that could put our lives in harm's way. The prospect of giving our lives at such a young age was a sobering reality.

We were given a brief period of time off between graduation and reporting to officer training. This pause between the structured life of the Academy and the structured life of the military felt strange for its lack of structure. I used it to reflect, gather my thoughts, and appreciate everything that had led up to that moment. I reconnected with family and friends, took some time to travel, partied a bit, and relaxed.

Although I didn't have much money, I had time. I was also about to start receiving my pay as a second lieutenant, which meant I didn't have to worry about making my funds last indefinitely. I decided to use my vacation time to travel, taking advantage of the "Space Available" option on military flights to visit Europe and the West Coast. It was a cost-effective way to unwind before stepping into my position as an officer. I was aware the job ahead wouldn't be easy, but I was ready and felt a deep sense of peace, knowing I was starting this journey well prepared and well rested. That short time off provided me the clarity and focus I needed before reporting to Officer Basic Course for a few months of additional training prior to my first official military assignment.

OFFICER BASIC COURSE

Graduation from Armor Officer Basic Course—Real Tank Dogs

From West Point, those of us who joined the military went next to Officer Basic Course. This course prepared second lieutenants to become full-time platoon leaders by helping them specialize in their chosen branch of military service. In my case, that was Armor.

New Armor officers spent their course time learning about equipment, military tactics, and any other knowledge necessary to lead soldiers and prepare for real military situations. For me, the focus of my Officer Basic Course was mastering battle tanks and maneuvering my tank platoon. Graduates were expected to have both technical and tactical proficiency with tanks to earn their commissions.

The course taught me everything I needed to know about operating and commanding tanks. I spent hours learning how to maneuver these massive machines, studying the complexities of tank warfare, and practicing how to communicate with my crew under high-pressure situations. However, I wasn't just responsible for the operation of one tank—I was to also command three others and ensure we all moved as a cohesive unit.

We trained to work as a team, practicing giving and following orders accurately because there is no room for mistakes in battle. During our training, we simulated real battlefield scenarios. It was thrilling to be in the driver's seat, feeling the power of the tank as we practiced maneuvers and strategies. Yet, it was also humbling. The weight of responsibility hit me as we were constantly reminded that, one day, real lives would depend on our decisions. This sobering thought occupied my mind throughout the course.

This focused training prepared me to be a soldier and lead others in combat. Nothing could better equip an army officer for the practical realities of military life than this course and the outstanding noncommissioned officers, with their significant years of experience, who dedicated their time and energy to us young lieutenants.

My Officer Basic Course was held in Fort Knox, Kentucky, and lasted three months. I was part of a cohort of twenty-three, all newly commissioned lieutenants eager to prove ourselves. We came from different backgrounds and experiences but shared the same goal: to become capable officers ready to command our platoons. From the very first day, we were thrown into the deep end, learning everything there was to know about tank warfare and leadership in combat.

Our training started with the basics, such as how to operate a tank, move it across rugged terrain, and handle the weapons systems. Each day was filled with drills and simulations. Hours in the classroom learning strategy and tactics were followed by even more time in the field putting that knowledge to the test, often against one another in simulated combat. The course trained us to evolve from individual lieutenants into tank platoon leaders, commanding other tanks alongside our own. The focus was on coordination, communication, and making quick decisions under pressure.

Training was mentally and physically exhausting, so naturally, my buddies and I sometimes needed a break to unwind. On those days, my friend Cedric Bray and I would head to Louisville, Kentucky, to catch a movie, visit a bar, or go to a dance club. After all, everyone needs some downtime to refresh and recharge.

Unbeknownst to us, we became the talk of the class for our ability to go out multiple nights a week and still excel in our training exercises. Despite being young and eager to enjoy life after West Point, we knew we needed to focus on our training because mistakes could cost lives—either during training or in real combat with these powerful machines.

Our Officer Basic Course class bonded as a cohort over those few short months. We supported each other through tough times, shared advice, and pushed each other to improve. By the end of the course, we were no longer just peers; we were tankers. Little did I know then that many of us would continue to support one another in future combat situations.

DOGFACE SOLDIER OF THE 3RD INFANTRY DIVISION

After training at Fort Knox, Kentucky, I was assigned to the army's 3rd Infantry Division at Fort Stewart in Hinesville, Georgia, known as the Marne Division because of its heroic actions during the Second Battle of the Marne in World War I. The unit's bravery in halting the German offensive and launching a successful counterattack along the Marne River earned them this nickname, which epitomizes their courage and resilience in battle.

Being a combat arms officer in the Marne Division was a significant step, and I was eager to join my unit. Fort Knox had prepared me well, and I felt confident everything I had learned was about to be put into practice. Upon my arrival, I was assigned to Alpha Company in the 3-69 Armor Battalion, whose motto was "Speed and power." The unit immediately designated me a tank platoon leader.

The day I arrived in Georgia, I felt a mix of pride and anxiety. Walking onto the base, I observed soldiers going about their duties, tanks lined up, and the constant hum of military life. It was surreal to think I was now responsible for leading a platoon. Each soldier under my command had their own unique experiences, and I was excited to train alongside them. Being their leader meant I had to earn their trust and respect. As Major John Roseborough often reminded us, respect is not given; it is earned. I never forgot this lesson. Even though the army had made me the platoon leader, I felt the need to prove to my soldiers that I was worthy of this designation.

As part of a rapid deployment force, we always needed to be battle ready. Many of the men looked to me for guidance, and I needed to approach my role with both confidence and humility. I had learned during my training to spend time with my soldiers, acquainting myself with each person's strengths to ensure a smooth team dynamic. As a tank platoon leader, I was responsible for overseeing fifteen men and four M1A2 battle tanks, each valued at $7 million. I was only twenty-two years old, and the weight of leadership began to set in.

On my first day, my commander, Captain Bill Papanastasiou, called me into his office. He was a no-nonsense leader, a sharp West Point graduate with years of experience. He wasted no time in laying out his expectations. "Lieutenant," he said, looking me straight in the eye, "your first assignment is to get all your platoon's equipment laid out and take inventory. You'll sign for it, and you're responsible for every piece from then on. If anything goes missing, it's on you."

I nodded, recognizing this as my first real leadership test. The next day, I gathered my platoon and informed them I would be holding an inspection to catalog 100 percent of our equipment. We spent hours laying out every single item on the checklist. The soldiers were efficient—they had done this before—but it was my responsibility to ensure everything was present and accounted for. We checked radios, weapons, ammunition, night-vision goggles, spare tank parts, and more. There were hundreds of items, and I had to confirm each one was there.

As we conducted the inventory, I quickly realized, as the captain had hinted, that some items were missing. A few radios were unaccounted for, and some tools could not be placed. "Welcome to the military," Staff Sergeant Greene said with a smirk. Sergeant Greene was also a reverend at a local Baptist church, and it always sounded like he was singing the gospel when he spoke. "Things always go missing, sir. No big deal, sir," he added, shooting a wink in my direction. However, it was a problem, and as the platoon leader, it became my problem. I gathered the men together and said, "Alright, listen up. We're missing some equipment, and I need all of you to help track it down. I'm not signing off on anything until we account for everything."

Picture me, baby-faced with a bright gold bar, facing soldiers with ages ranging from seventeen to forty and trying to establish myself as a no-nonsense leader. Some of my soldiers had been in the military for nearly as long as I had been alive and had real combat experience, which was intimidating. Therefore, I needed to navigate my leadership approach cautiously until I got my footing and we got to know each other better. I knew this would take some time.

Just then, one of the young sergeants, Sergeant Gronchowski, probably in his mid-twenties, grinned and said, "Hey, LT! We've got it. Don't worry about it; it's all good." The others laughed, and I could feel the playful tension in the air. They were testing me, seeing how I would handle it. I chuckled along with them and replied, "I trust you, but I need to verify that the equipment exists—nothing personal." I could hear Major Roseborough's words of wisdom echoing in my head: "Trust but verify." I knew I couldn't just take their word for it; I had to see the gear for myself, or I would be the one to pay if something was missing later.

I then said, "Hey, Third Platoon, we're a team, and teams support each other. As such, I need you to support me by getting this equipment laid out. The sooner we get this done, the sooner we can all go home." They hesitated for a moment, but I kept my tone light, making it clear I wanted to work with them, not against them. The power struggle was palpable, but I stood in that motor pool, with the Savannah, Georgia, sun beaming down on me, determined to see every last piece of equipment.

Eventually, I outlasted them, and Staff Sergeant Greene, a squad leader, said, "Alright, sir, I'll get the guys to bring it all out." Slowly but surely, the rest of the team followed, and soon, we had everything laid out in front of us—radios, weapons, spare parts, all the gear I had to sign for. I checked each item, ensured everything was there, and thanked them for their help.

This moment taught me something important. As a young leader, I had to show my team I had conviction and wasn't going to take shortcuts. It wasn't just about commanding; it was about demonstrating that I wasn't going to back down or get upset but had the confidence to insist on doing the right thing.

Once we laid out all the equipment and I had everything listed, it was time for my next big challenge: getting to know my soldiers. My platoon sergeant, Sergeant First Class (SFC) Shillingford, approached me with a knowing smile as I wrapped up the inventory. "Alright, sir," he said, his arms crossed. "Now comes the fun part. You need to get to know your team. They need to know who you are, and you need to know who they are. Trust me, it makes everything easier."

"Yeah, I get that," I replied, feeling the weight of the responsibility. "But how do I even start?" SFC Shillingford chuckled and, in his light Caribbean accent, said, "Just start chatting. It doesn't have to be formal. Ask them about their backgrounds, what they enjoy doing when not in uniform, or even their favorite foods. Make it personal. If they see you as someone they can talk to, they'll be more willing to follow your lead."

Taking his advice to heart, I gathered the team around. "Alright, everyone," I began, trying to keep my voice upbeat. "I know this is a bit of a change, but I'd like to take a few minutes to get to know each of you. Let's start with something easy. What's your favorite food? I'm a big fan of pizza myself."

One of the younger soldiers, a private with an eager smile, chimed in first. "I love tacos! Can't beat taco Tuesday!" The group laughed, and I could feel the tension easing. I responded, "Taco Tuesday sounds great! I'll bring the toppings next week. Who's next?"

An older sergeant spoke up, crossing his arms. "You know, Lieutenant, we don't get a lot of pizza around here. You might have to treat us all to that soon."

"Deal!" I laughed, trying to keep the mood light. "What about you, Sergeant?"

He paused before replying, "I'm a steak guy. But I also have a soft spot for barbecue. Do you have any skills on the grill?"

"Of course, I'm from the South, but I could always use some tips," I responded.

The conversation flowed easily from there, with each team member sharing their favorite foods, hobbies, and even a few fun stories from their time in the military. As we talked, I noticed everyone slowly opening up, offering more than just their food preferences. The private who loved tacos revealed that his dad was a rear admiral in the navy, and the older soldier told tales of his years in service, sprinkling in humor about the mishaps he had experienced along the way. By the end of our informal chat, I felt I had a better understanding of who each of them was outside of his uniform.

Knowing your team inside and out is vital, especially as a lieutenant at the garrison or home base. Some of my primary responsibilities included confirming maintenance was done on our equipment, ensuring soldiers had everything they needed, and helping those facing financial troubles navigate the necessary paperwork.

A lot of administrative work came with the job, and it would be easy to fall behind if I wasn't careful. At garrison, the relationship between a lieutenant and a sergeant was crucial. My platoon sergeant and I often joked that the relationship between a lieutenant and a sergeant was like the one between a husband and wife. Everything ran smoothly if the lieutenant–sergeant connection was strong, was built on mutual respect, and both were aligned in their approach to "raising the children." From the start, I knew I had to establish that bond with my platoon sergeant.

During our early days together, I made it a point to communicate openly and honestly with SFC Shillingford. One afternoon, after a long training day, I called him into my office. "Hey, can we talk for a minute?" I asked, inviting him to take a seat.

"Sure, sir. What's on your mind?" he replied, looking attentive.

"I just want to ensure we're on the same page," I said. "I know I'm new to all this, and I value your experience. I want to support you and the team in any way I can."

He smiled, appreciating the gesture. "I understand. We need to communicate. If we work together, we can resolve many issues before they become problems."

"Exactly," I said, feeling relieved. "If you ever see something that needs my attention, just let me know. I want you to feel comfortable sharing your thoughts. My goal is to create an environment where we can be honest and straightforward with each other."

"Deal," he said, nodding. "I appreciate how you've stepped in to help soldiers with administrative issues like finance and citizenship paperwork.

It shows the platoon that you care about their well-being." I smiled and thanked him for his support.

I also took the time to check in with each of my soldiers individually. I wanted them to feel heard and valued, just as I did with my sergeant. One time, I noticed one of the younger soldiers looking stressed at meetings. I pulled him aside after a meeting. "Hey, is everything okay?" I asked.

"Honestly, sir, I'm having trouble keeping up with my bills," he admitted, looking slightly embarrassed.

I reassured him, "You're not alone. Let's get you the help you need." After reviewing his files, I discovered he had an extremely high interest rate on a car loan from a dealership known to take advantage of soldiers. I took his paperwork to the finance office, secured him a fair rate, and reported the dealership for price gouging unsuspecting soldiers. At West Point, we weren't educated on these real-life issues, but we were trained to adapt to any situation.

The open dialogue I established with my team helped foster a culture where the soldiers knew I supported them. As a result, they felt more comfortable sharing their concerns with me, and I could address many of their issues before they escalated into more significant problems.

KNOW YOUR PEOPLE

People often think military personnel follow orders simply because they must. While that might be true to some extent, this mindset leads to "utter obedience." If you manage your team for utter obedience, whether in the military or civilian world, they'll do exactly what you ask and nothing more. They'll turn off that one hose or fix the one PowerPoint but won't address the other obvious issues related to the one you asked them to solve. This is a real problem, especially in a combat situation. You need soldiers who will go the extra mile, not just do the bare minimum. A commanding officer or sergeant breathing down your neck is not enough to inspire excellence. Leadership is about building relationships and trust. To lead effectively, you must genuinely know your people and take care of them. You need to dedicate time to understanding their strengths, weaknesses, and motivators.

During my early days as a tank platoon leader, I learned how important it was to connect with my team on a personal level. Mutual respect is the foundation of a strong team—this was the most important lesson I learned as a new leader. When soldiers feel respected and valued, they develop a sense of loyalty that drives them to go above and beyond.

I remember a training exercise where we faced a simulated attack. It was chaotic, with tanks moving and orders being shouted. One of my soldiers, who had previously hesitated, took the initiative. He quickly identified an issue with one of our tanks and sprang into action. Instead of waiting for me to tell him what to do, he stepped up and directed his fellow soldiers to help. "We need to fix this now! Let's get to it!" he yelled. That's the kind of response you want to cultivate in your team. Every team needs individuals who take the initiative because they care about their comrades and the mission.

Every morning, my platoon followed a strict routine without fail. We gathered as a group to exercise, starting with a run. It was more than just a workout; it became a time for bonding and fun. As we ran, we sang military songs, our voices rising in unison. There was a special pride in knowing we could maintain an incredible pace while running past other units. This shared experience made us feel strong and connected.

The physical fitness training didn't just keep us in shape; it also built up our confidence. Running together each day inspired a strong team spirit. We cheered each other on and pushed one another to do our best.

Our first significant graded and simulated training event took place at the Joint Readiness Training Center in Fort Polk, Louisiana. We were training for a deployment on a peacekeeping mission. This training stripped away formalities and revealed our true selves under pressure. During this time, my platoon learned to rely on one another. When someone stumbled, another stepped in to help. I began to understand my soldiers on a deeper level and recognized those who had the sharpest instincts in stressful situations, who were the quickest on their feet, and who were the most dependable when things got tough. The training showcased their abilities, competencies, and depths of character.

That phase of training built a foundation of trust within our platoon.

We would need that foundation as we received orders to deploy to Kosovo in support of a NATO peacekeeping mission in the region. More than ever, we needed to function as a cohesive team rather than a group of individuals.

CHAPTER 6 TRIGGERS

I can identify several triggers that arose during this transformative period of my life. These moments, while shaping me as a leader and soldier, also planted seeds of mental strain that I would carry forward.

- One significant trigger was the overwhelming sense of responsibility I felt upon becoming a tank platoon leader. At just twenty-two years old, I was entrusted with the lives of fifteen soldiers and millions of dollars' worth of equipment. The weight of accountability was immense, especially during my first inventory inspection. The pressure to ensure every piece of equipment was accounted for coupled with the subtle power struggle with my soldiers caused mental strain. I remember standing in the motor pool, under the blazing Savannah sun, determined to prove myself while feeling the tension of being tested by seasoned soldiers. The fear of failure and need to earn respect created a constant undercurrent of stress.
- Another trigger was the realization of the life-and-death stakes of my role. During the Officer Basic Course, the thought that real lives would depend on my decisions in combat was sobering and constant. This awareness weighed heavily on me, especially during simulated battlefield scenarios. The mental toll of knowing that mistakes could cost lives was something I couldn't shake, even during moments of camaraderie or downtime.
- My transition from the structured life at West Point to the real-world responsibilities of military service was another trigger. While I felt prepared, the abrupt shift brought a sense of uncertainty. The brief pause before reporting to my first assignment allowed me to reflect, but it also amplified the reality of what lay ahead. The looming prospect of deployment and inherent dangers of military life added to my anxiety.

- Building relationships with my soldiers was both rewarding and challenging. While I understood the importance of connecting with them on a personal level, the process of earning their trust and navigating their diverse personalities was mentally exhausting. Moments like helping a young soldier with financial troubles highlighted the real-life issues that weren't included in my West Point training. The emotional burden of addressing their concerns while maintaining my own composure was a quiet strain.
- Finally, the constant need to prove myself as a leader was a recurring trigger. Whether it was during training exercises, bonding activities, or formal inspections, I felt the pressure to demonstrate my competence and earn respect. The fear of being perceived as inadequate or inexperienced lingered in the back of my mind, driving me to push myself harder.

These triggers—responsibility, life-and-death stakes, transitions, relationship building, and the pressure to prove myself—were pivotal moments that shaped me but also contributed to underlying mental strain. While I didn't fully recognize their impact at the time, they were the foundation of future challenges I would face.

CHAPTER 7

NEXT STOP, KOSOVO

BEFORE COMING TO MY UNIT, I KNEW WE HAD AN UPCOMING deployment to Kosovo for a peacekeeping mission. As the days stretched on, my anticipation of deploying grew. It was early 2001, and Kosovo was the most critical military mission taking place at the time. I experienced a strange mix of emotions: excitement, nervousness, and many other feelings that cannot be described.

I had spent so long preparing for this moment, yet the waiting was still a test I did not have all the answers to. My thoughts often drifted to the unknowns: what challenges awaited me, and how would I deal with the complexities of real-world military operations? But beneath the uncertainty was a promise I had made to myself to keep growing. I trusted my training, my instincts, and the bonds I had built with my platoon. Whatever lay ahead, I knew we would face it together and emerge victorious.

Deployment is unlike any other job. It's not a routine where you clock in at 9:00 a.m. and out at 5:00 p.m., returning to the comfort of your bed every evening. It's a complete and often jarring departure from everyday life. Once you're deployed, you don't come home until the mission is over, whatever "over" might mean.

One thing that lingers in an army officer's thoughts is that you might not come home. Deployment strips away the everyday luxuries we often take for granted, such as waking up to familiar surroundings, sharing a meal with loved ones, and even the simple reassurance of knowing that at the end of a hard day, home is waiting.

For many, deployment is not an exciting prospect at all. Others look forward to deploying and the significant tax breaks and deployment salary bonuses that come with it. Even so, for every soldier, some fear and dread accompany deployment.

For seasoned soldiers, deployment is a heavy weight to bear. They carry with them the stories of their past missions, the ones they are willing to share and the ones they will take to their graves. They have seen the realities of deployment, such as long nights, dangerous missions, the endless grind of routine, and the constant tension of being on high alert.

The feeling was entirely different for someone like me, a young soldier fresh out of training, eager to prove my worth. Deployment was the badge of honor I craved, the ultimate test of everything I had worked for. It was the opportunity to show my peers, superiors, and, most importantly, myself that I belonged. I wanted to meaningfully contribute to the mission. More than anything, I wanted to prove I had what it took to lead, serve, and succeed in the military.

West Point meticulously trained us for scenarios we might face in the field. But none of it could replicate the realities of deployment, like being away from home, cut off from the life you once knew, with every decision carrying a significant weight, including life and death. As such, part of me was excited to deploy, while another part seriously questioned my choice to join the military. I asked myself questions like, "What would it feel like serving in a foreign country? Would I freeze up under pressure or rise to the occasion?"

Back at headquarters, I often overheard the senior sergeants talking to each other about their past deployments or referring to particular incidents they took part in or wished they had. They never gave away much, just coded words and inside jokes that seemed to carry entire stories behind them.

Sometimes, they would sit in quiet reflection, their expressions betraying a depth of emotion no words could capture, such as remembering a comrade and friend who died while serving their country. It made me wonder what my story would be. Would I come back with cryptic anecdotes or return silent? I didn't know, but I was ready, or at least, I thought I was.

The truth is that no amount of training can prepare you for deployment; this is something you keep hearing in the military. Deployment is a leap into the unknown, testing your physical and tactical skills, mental health, and emotional resilience. It is a reminder that in the military, you do not just wear the uniform; you live it, breathe it, and sometimes sacrifice more than you ever expected for it. For all the fears I carried, one thing was sure: I was determined to find out what I was made of.

FINDING MY PLACE

Before I received my first deployment order, I faced many challenges, but the most significant was finding my place. As a new officer in combat arms, I quickly realized the importance of paving the way for future officers who aspire to lead. My goal became clear: I wanted to do my part to ensure the next generation of young officers, regardless of background, feel supported and represented.

Forming relationships with my fellow officers was crucial. In the military, camaraderie is vital, but it doesn't happen overnight. As a new lieutenant, I had to prove my worth and earn my place. Acceptance required more than just showing up in uniform; it demanded genuine engagement and connection.

My peers had diverse backgrounds and experiences, and many did not attend West Point. I recognized the need to meet them where they were, breaking down barriers and fostering open communication. Often, this meant overcoming preconceived notions—especially the stigma that can come with attending the Academy. I aimed to demonstrate I was eager to earn their respect, not just rely on my rank.

While investing time in building trust with my colleagues, I discovered that my unique perspective allowed me to connect deeply with my soldiers. Many of them came from working-class environments, grappling with struggles for respect and acknowledgment. I sought to create an atmosphere where they could share their experiences and feel valued.

However, balancing these relationships was challenging. While I connected well with my soldiers, I needed to build rapport with my peers. There was a persistent pressure to prove myself—not just as an officer but as a role model for future leaders. Any misstep felt magnified, as I was aware my actions could influence how others view those who might follow in my footsteps.

I carried the responsibility of representation, understanding that my success could help shape opportunities for aspiring officers. This realization became both a burden and a motivator. I pushed myself to excel, striving to create an environment where the next young officer could thrive without the limitations I faced.

My journey to carve out a space for myself taught me about resilience and authenticity. More importantly, it instilled in me a commitment to support the next generation of leaders, ensuring they have the opportunities and encouragement needed to succeed. Each day, I fought not just for my place but for a path where future officers could find their own.

GUARDIANS OF PEACE

As the transport plane touched down in Kosovo, I was immediately struck by the stillness and calm of the area, which contrasted sharply with my expectations. From the air, the landscape appeared peaceful, with rolling hills and villages nestled in the valleys. However, once I stepped onto the ground, it became clear why the military presence was necessary.

Kosovo had endured horrors that are almost unimaginable. The genocide that scarred the region stemmed from historical animosity between Christians and Muslims, with each side perceiving the other as an existential threat. Families were displaced, entire communities destroyed, and the wounds—both physical and emotional—remained tender and raw. Our mission as peacekeepers was to ensure that these wounds did not reopen and to prevent further violence, fostering a space where dialogue, however fragile, could replace bloodshed.

Before deploying to Kosovo, my unit gained a new company commander: Captain Robert Dye. Captain Dye was the biggest Asian guy I had ever seen. He was six feet three inches tall and around 240 pounds, built like the tanks he commanded. He was interesting because he was half Asian and half rural Alabamian. A graduate of the University of Alabama, he was 100 percent Roll Tide. Most of the time, he communicated like a calm and orderly Asian businessman. However, when he got angry, his Southern Alabama trucker drawl would come out, and we lieutenants would run for cover. It was a privilege to serve with him.

Our task was not glamorous, but it was essential. The deployment of US Army troops to Kosovo was part of broader international efforts to restore peace, protect civilians, and facilitate the rebuilding of infrastructure and institutions after the conflict. The presence of US troops helped support the transition to a more stable and secure environment in the region.

We patrolled the villages, often walking the thin line between two opposing sides, ensuring tensions did not escalate into skirmishes. Part of our role involved mediation, where we facilitated meetings between local leaders, urging them to seek dialogue rather than confrontations. This was a challenging task.

Decades of mistrust and pain do not dissolve overnight, and there were moments it felt like we were asking the impossible. However, in those rare instances when progress was achieved—like when two leaders shook hands or a family was able to return home—all our efforts felt worthwhile.

Our primary responsibility in Kosovo involved setting up Traffic Control Points (TCPs), which were crucial for maintaining order and preventing the transport of illegal weapons or contraband. This meticulous work involved stopping vehicles at random checkpoints to inspect trunks, glove compartments, and even the spaces under car seats for anything suspicious. Most of the time, people were cooperative, though the tension in their eyes was unmistakable—they understood the stakes.

If we discovered weapons or other illegal items, we confiscated them and made arrests on the spot. While some drivers protested, the rules were clear, and we enforced them with a calm but firm approach, ensuring compliance.

While we were doing routine checks in Kosovo one day, we received an anonymous tip that a house in a nearby village was stockpiling weapons. The informant told us it could be an arsenal able to supply an entire militia. Now we weren't just doing routine TCP work anymore: We were on a mission to get those weapons.

We planned the operation meticulously, as per our training and operational procedures. We began by reviewing maps of the area and gathering as much intelligence as possible. My platoon and I moved out in the middle of the night to monitor the target location and collect intel on what was going into and coming out of the location, trying to get an idea of how weapons were changing hands and who the players were.

We gathered intelligence over three days, and on the third day, we moved out in a convoy at nightfall to make arrests. Our vehicles kicked up dust as we approached the target location. The air was thick with anticipation and fear that this could turn into something huge. We were ready, but there was always that sliver of doubt: What if things went wrong?

As we surrounded the house, the darkness seemed to close in around us. Flashlights flickered across the perimeter, and the sharp whispers of commands punctuated the silence. My heart raced as we prepared to breach the building.

The atmosphere was tense as we stormed into the dimly lit house. The air was heavy with the scent of sweat and anticipation. Suddenly, a blood-curdling scream pierced the silence, echoing through the halls. It sent a shiver down my spine, a stark reminder of the potential dangers lurking just out of sight.

I quickly signaled to my team, our instincts kicking in as we moved through the rooms with precision. The scream had broken the calm, but it had also ignited a fire within us. Voices erupted from the back of the house, angry and defiant. A group of individuals was gathered, and it was clear they were not going to go down without a fight.

"On the ground!" we shouted, our commands punctuated by the urgency of the moment. Chaos ensued as they resisted, shoving against one another, trying to make a break for it. But we were ready. Each member of my team moved to contain the situation, blocking exits and corralling those who dared to flee.

As we pushed through the throng, our eyes widened in shock at what we discovered. Hidden behind walls and tucked away in corners were dozens of weapons: rifles, handguns, and an alarming number of grenades. This was beyond what we had anticipated. Our mission had just escalated: We had uncovered a significant arsenal.

With each weapon we cataloged, the urgency grew. We worked methodically, confiscating everything while ensuring no one could make a move against us. We handcuffed the individuals one by one, their defiance fading as they realized the futility of their resistance.

Finally, the last of them was secured, and the house was quiet again, save for the soft clinking of metal and rustle of uniforms. As we stood among the confiscated weapons, a palpable sense of relief washed over us. We had averted a potential disaster, but the intensity of the moment weighed heavily on my mind.

This encounter reminded us all of the razor-thin line we walked daily, teetering between safety and chaos. The screams, the resistance, and the weapons were vivid embodiments of the challenges we faced, but today, we emerged victorious. The operation was a success, but the shadow of the night's events lingered, reminding us that there was always more work to be done.

Our duties did not end there. Occasionally, riots would break out, fueled by anger and resentment between the communities. These situations were some of the most challenging I faced. A sea of angry faces, voices raised in unison, rocks pelting our shields and riot gear, and much more. It was overwhelming to see people fight like that. Our job was to de-escalate and restore order without creating further violence. It required incredible restraint and composure.

THE WORLD CHANGES

Kosovo was a land of contrasts. There were moments of intense action, like the raid, where every second mattered and your training was all that stood between success and disaster. Then there were quieter days, where the real challenge was trying to tread the fragile relationships between people divided by years of hatred and violence. Each day brought something new.

One of the most critical aspects of our mission in Kosovo, beyond securing the peace, was ensuring daily life could go on for the people caught in the crossfire of the conflict. We had to oversee critical tasks like providing fresh water to communities, ensuring children could go to school, and helping families rebuild some semblance of normalcy. These were simple things on the surface, but they were monumental in a place scarred by genocide and violence.

The children stood out to me the most. Despite the tension surrounding them, these pure souls managed to smile, laugh, and play. Watching them run around barefoot, kicking a makeshift ball or chasing each other in games that needed no translation, was a sight that gave hope and optimism to many of us. Their joy was infectious, the kind that would cut through the gloom of broken buildings and fractured lives. It was humbling.

These kids, who had seen and endured more than any child should, still found reasons to laugh. It made our work feel worthwhile. If we could help preserve their innocence, even for a moment longer, the long days and sleepless nights would have been worth it.

During my time in Kosovo, I was the mayor of two towns: Pasjak and Brasaljce. The residents of both faced a significant challenge: They had to travel to a single location to access fresh water. This became an integral part of their daily lives. Every morning, families would gather at the water source, carrying buckets and containers to collect the precious water they needed for cooking, cleaning, and drinking. I witnessed the struggles of the townspeople firsthand, and it was clear how vital this resource was to their survival.

These were tough days for everyone involved. I remember walking with some of the villagers as they made their way to the water source. One elderly man, his face weathered by time, looked at me and said, "Water is life here. Without it, we are nothing." His words struck a chord with me, highlighting the gravity of the situation. I felt a profound responsibility to help improve their access to this essential resource.

This situation forced me to learn valuable lessons in planning and problem-solving. I had to organize daily patrols to ensure the safety of the townspeople as they collected water. I mapped out routes to ensure everyone could access the water without threats. My land-navigation skills improved tremendously as I became more familiar with the terrain. I often told my team, "Stay close, and let's ensure everyone gets there and back safely."

Communication also played a crucial role in my duties. I had to engage with the villagers and my fellow soldiers to coordinate efforts effectively. I learned how to listen carefully to the townspeople's needs and understand their concerns about the water supply. As I worked alongside the villagers, I realized being a leader isn't just about making decisions; it's about being there for others and understanding their needs.

My platoon's workdays in Kosovo were grueling, operating two twelve-hour shifts seven days a week. To ensure continuous coverage, the platoon was divided into two teams, each handling one shift. As the officer-in-charge, my responsibilities didn't end when one team clocked out. I had to supervise both shifts, ensuring everything ran smoothly, whether it was monitoring checkpoints, resolving disputes, or addressing the soldiers' needs. There were days I barely had time to sit down, moving from one task to the next, juggling the mission's needs and my team's well-being.

The physical and mental toll was enormous. I often worked well beyond my shift to provide support where it was needed most. The soldiers in my platoon were my responsibility, and I felt the weight of that responsibility daily. Whether it was a logistical issue, a soldier struggling with homesickness, or a mission requiring immediate action, I was the one they turned to. Leading them meant being present, even when I was exhausted.

Eating meals together in makeshift mess halls, swapping stories during the small moments of downtime, or simply laughing at the absurdity of the situation kept us going. These moments built trust and unity within the platoon, the kind of bond you can only forge under pressure. Kosovo was a test of endurance, not just in the physical sense but emotionally and mentally as well.

The evolution of my military leadership was eye-opening for me. My journey from a newly commissioned officer to a deployed leader was marked by growth, challenge, and, most importantly, the strengthening of bonds within my unit. We didn't start as a close-knit team, which was alarming for me at the time, but we became one unit eventually through shared trials and experiences forged by training, hardship, and the missions that lay ahead. By the time our deployment ended, I knew I wasn't leading a group of strangers anymore. I was leading a team that could rely on each other, no matter what came next. When the deployment finally came to an end, the familiar weight of exhaustion and experience settled on all of us, though there was a sense of relief in the air.

Unfortunately, during our time in Kosovo, September 11 happened. We knew we were leaving the peacekeeping behind at that point and returning to the United States to prepare for combat.

It was one of the most challenging yet rewarding times of my life. So much had happened in such a short period. I smiled faintly, reflecting on everything we had been through together.

"Well, folks, I can't believe it's over. Landing in Kosovo feels like it was a lifetime ago, but also like we just got here," I said, breaking the silence.

One of my favorite soldiers, seated next to me, grinned. "No kidding, sir. I thought those shifts would never end. Now I'm unsure what to do with myself without the sound of checkpoint arguments or kids running around yelling at us in Albanian."

"Don't forget the rocks," one soldier added to the conversation.

I chuckled, remembering the moments of chaos. Our training was put to the test many times in Kosovo. We had accomplished the mission we were tasked to do. Now, we had to refocus our efforts on reintegrating into our families and getting our minds ready for a possible combat deployment to the Middle East in support of the global war on terrorism. These were both exciting and dangerous times, but each experience made us better individuals and teammates.

Through my experiences in Kosovo, I learned effective leadership encompasses much more than just tactical training; it fundamentally revolves around building trust and camaraderie with my team. Embracing adaptability and being open to new experiences became essential to navigating the uncertainties of deployment. The human aspects of leadership—such as empathy, resilience, and the ability to inspire—proved vital in fostering a cohesive unit.

I discovered that personal connections and shared experiences significantly strengthen team dynamics, even in challenging circumstances. Moreover, my commitment to ongoing growth and a strong sense of duty to my soldiers underscored the importance of self-improvement and support. Ultimately, these lessons highlighted the multifaceted nature of military leadership and the profound impact of nurturing relationships within a team.

CHAPTER 7 TRIGGERS

I can identify several significant triggers that arose during this time that not only shaped my military journey but also potentially influenced my mental health in the long term.

- The overwhelming anticipation of deployment inspired many new thoughts and emotions. I was filled with excitement mixed with nervousness, a duality that left me feeling vulnerable. The lead-up to the mission was marked by constant thoughts spiraling into the unknown: What challenges awaited me? How would I cope? And, most importantly, would I be able to perform under pressure? These questions created a mental burden that began to weigh heavily on me. The fear of failure became a persistent background hum, triggering anxieties I would later struggle to put aside.
- Another poignant trigger was the stark realization of what deployment truly meant. The transition from a structured home life to the unpredictable nature of military operations was jarring. The thought of not coming home was a frightening possibility I had to confront regularly. Each time I considered the luxuries of home—simple moments like sharing a meal or being enveloped in familiarity—I felt a wave of sadness wash over me. It made me acutely aware of what I had to sacrifice, stoking feelings of isolation and melancholy that lingered in

my thoughts. The uncertainty stripped away my comforts and further tested my resilience.
- The discourse among seasoned soldiers also served as a significant trigger. Listening to their vague yet powerful storytelling created a unique pressure. They spoke in cryptic terms about harrowing experiences, and I found myself grappling with an intense desire to belong and be part of that world. However, their quiet reflections often hinted at deep-rooted pain and loss, sparking my own fears about the emotional toll of deployment. Would I also have stories laden with grief? This contemplation of my potential future weighed on me, casting shadows on my eagerness to prove myself.
- It was particularly revealing to hear discussions among comrades who had experienced loss while serving. Those conversations fostered an environment of silent fears, one that most soldiers carried yet seldom spoke openly about. I found myself wondering if I would come back with my own scars—both seen and unseen. Each time these thoughts arose, I felt increased anxiety and uncertainty regarding my mental fortitude and emotional resilience.

The constant mental tug-of-war between excitement and dread kept me on edge. I was ready to prove my worth, but could I handle the emotional aftermath if things went wrong? As much as I yearned for deployment to solidify my place in the military, another part of me questioned whether I was truly equipped for the realities I would soon face. These conflicting feelings began to foster self-doubt and could, potentially, have led to deeper mental health issues.

Ultimately, the blend of anticipation, fear of the unknown, weight of loss, and pressure to perform were all potent triggers throughout this chapter. They provided a glimpse into the mental health challenges I would face and have since continued to navigate. These experiences illuminated the complexities of military life and serve as a reminder that the battle for mental resilience often begins long before the mission does. Each trigger I encountered added layers to my understanding of what I would face—not just on the battlefield but within my own mind as well.

CHAPTER 8

FROM PEACEKEEPING TO COMBAT

The cavalrymen of Charlie Troop, 1st US Cavalry "Cutthroat Recon"

There were many things I loved about being an officer in the military. One was that our lives were indeed full of surprises. No two days were similar, and that filled my life with unexpected events, challenges, and experiences that shaped me in ways I could have never imagined. The unpredictability kept things exciting and supplied a constant source of adrenaline.

During my time in Kosovo, I learned to value the resilience exhibited by the local people. They inhabited a place torn apart by violence and faced hardships with incredible strength and courage. Their determination taught me to push through my struggles.

That said, the peacekeeping mission in Kosovo did have challenges, and many moments made me miss being comfortable in the United States. When I received the order to return home, a mix of emotions washed over me. I was excited to return home, but I was also sad to leave behind the neighborhoods and people I had protected in Kosovo. I had this strange sense of wanting to continue serving the people of Kosovo.

Kosovo taught me lessons no textbook or training exercise could have, and I am forever grateful for having had the opportunity to support others in making a better life for themselves. I felt supremely ready to lead America's sons and daughters on our next adventure, wherever that was.

I returned from Kosovo in October 2001. We all knew the peacekeeping phase of deployments was over and the 3rd Infantry Division would quickly need to prepare for combat operations abroad.

I was no longer the same person. My experiences in Kosovo had profoundly changed me. I had grown stronger, not just physically but mentally and emotionally. I carried with me a newfound gratitude for the freedom and prosperity we enjoy in the United States of America and a certainty that if I lived with a purpose, nothing could truly stop me from accomplishing my goals. Additionally, I had learned that true leadership is about serving others and staying calm in the face of adversity. When I finally arrived in Savannah, Georgia, I was no longer the same naive military officer or overly enthusiastic leader I had once been. My experiences during my time away had significantly changed me.

A month after returning home, I was promoted to first lieutenant and received orders for a new assignment as a light cavalry scout. I would serve as the platoon leader for our Brigade Reconnaissance Troop, also known as Charlie Troop, 1st Cavalry. It was an honor to be selected for this highly sought-after position, as there were only two slots available within the entire brigade for infantry and armor lieutenants.

At that time, General Vincent Brooks was in command of the 1st Brigade, 3rd Infantry Division, and I was excited for the opportunity to serve as the forward eyes and ears of one of the army's most distinguished colonels, who later became a four-star general. I had met both Colin Powell and "Stormin" Norman Schwarzkopf after their military careers, but this was a chance to follow orders directly from an up-and-coming army legend.

A light cavalry brigade reconnaissance scout gathers intelligence on enemy movements and positions. This involves conducting patrols, observing the terrain, and reporting to the brigade commander details of the enemy and battlefield. Reconnaissance scouts often operate behind enemy lines; light scouts have limited armor and supplies. As such, they must use speed and agility to gather vital information that helps shape the brigade's tactical decisions.

Additionally, at times, light scouts must engage in combat operations to disrupt and delay enemy forces. They are sometimes the "speed bump" used to slow enemy advancement until larger forces arrive to lead the assault.

I was humbled when the commanding officers selected me to become a brigade scout. This meant I was one of the top lieutenants in the brigade and the higher-ups believed I had the physical, mental, and tactical ability to execute above and beyond on the battlefield.

When I arrived at Charlie Troop, it was like drinking through a fire hose trying to learn all the scouting techniques, such as elite map reading, setting up hidden watch positions to peek at the enemy, and understanding terrain to gain a tactical advantage.

This new role was not for the meek. Rumors circulated that our brigade would deploy to Afghanistan just a few months after my return from Kosovo, but that deployment did not happen. Anticipating combat on the horizon, I requested to attend the Scout Leaders Course to learn advanced scouting techniques, as I wanted to give my unit the best chance of success.

The United States Army Scout Leaders Course is a specialized training program designed to prepare soldiers for roles as reconnaissance scouts. The course includes intensive instruction in various areas, such as reconnaissance tactics, surveillance, target acquisition, and intelligence gathering. Its purpose is to enhance a soldier's ability to operate effectively in dynamic and challenging environments by utilizing advanced skills in navigation and stealth. The course consists of both classroom sessions and simulated combat missions, providing soldiers with the expertise needed to support their units in successful reconnaissance operations.

The training at the Scout Leaders Course was intense, with the graduation rate hovering around 65 percent at the time. During the first few weeks, we focused on classroom work covering tactical map reading, superior positioning, command and control, and several other critical topics, on which we were tested. Failing a test meant failing the course, and the instructors took pride in their craft, readily failing students, particularly officers.

After the classroom sessions, we moved to the field—essentially the woods—to simulate combat. We had to apply everything we had learned during the simulations of real-world scout missions. Additionally, everyone's leadership skills were tested. Each class member had the opportunity to lead; if you could not maintain effective command and control, the instructors would fail you and send you home that day.

Another challenge that made this course particularly tough was sleep deprivation. I'm not sure if every scout class experienced this, but our instructors had us conduct eighteen to twenty hours of combat simulations followed by a two-hour after-action review to discuss the mission's positives and negatives. After that, we were given only two to four hours to sleep, which was often less because we had to set up our sleeping areas. Some of us figured out that we could take our time setting up our sleep site to avoid having to lie down. However, the instructors caught on and ordered us to lie down. As soon as I fell asleep, I had to get back up to clean up my sleeping area and report back to headquarters for the next mission briefing.

The good news for me was that by this point in my military career, I had completed hundreds of real and simulated missions. My time in Kosovo had honed my map-reading skills and my ability to interpret a mission. When my mission came up, I knew better than to keep all the information centralized. I briefed each squad leader and, even better, provided them with my "commander's intent," which essentially outlines what needs to be accomplished during the mission (i.e., the mission's goal) even if things go awry. This short statement helps keep soldiers at all levels focused on the objective.

By empowering my team, I successfully completed my mission and earned the status of class leader. In this role, I made it my goal to help other soldiers who lacked my leadership experience pass the course. A few of those individuals have since retired as command sergeants major, while others have achieved the rank of colonel or general.

THE SPUR RIDE

After returning to my unit from the Scout Leaders Course, I walked with a newfound confidence, convinced I was the next coming of General Patton of reconnaissance scouting. However, my senior noncommissioned officers weren't impressed. They quickly informed me that I couldn't be considered a faithful cavalry scout until I participated in a spur ride and earned my spurs.

A spur ride is a tradition in cavalry units involving a series of tests a soldier must pass to earn their silver spurs, a prestigious symbol of membership in the cavalry. Our spur ride lasted twenty-four hours, during which we had to endure both emotional stressors and physical challenges while simulating combat scenarios. We began the day with a twelve-mile ruck march carrying fifty pounds of gear, which we had to complete within three hours. Upon finishing the ruck march, we were immediately sent out on tests of our physical and mental capabilities. One of the highlights of the mental testing involved disassembling and reassembling several weapons while blindfolded. Meanwhile, the current spur holders barbequed delicious steaks nearby, taunting us with the tempting aroma.

Many soldiers dropped out during the spur ride, but as a seasoned first lieutenant, I wasn't about to let my soldiers see me quit, so I persevered! By the end of the twenty-four hours, I had earned my silver spurs and Stetson. This accomplishment demonstrated my readiness, resilience, and commitment to teamwork to my soldiers. I believe it also earned me greater respect from them, as they recognized my dedication to the cavalry community. Scouts out!

No sooner had I returned from scout leader training and completed my spur ride than my unit was assigned another opportunity to bond: desert warfare training in the Mojave Desert, also known as the US Army's National Training Center (NTC).

Upon our arrival at NTC, we struggled to operate effectively as a team. We made several significant errors, such as departing late for missions, missing refueling points, and failing to establish proper radio contact with higher command. However, there were some bright spots at the platoon level; several members of my platoon received Army Commendation Medals on the spot for locating and destroying the enemy's reserve force. Nonetheless, we won and lost as a team, and a few individuals receiving medals could not distract from the fact that the rest of the company might be lost in combat. The most critical issue we had to address was ensuring our headquarters unit maintained tight control over resupply, command, and communication.

Our overall unit suffered significant losses against the simulated opposition force on multiple occasions. After one of our long missions at the training center, we were ordered by higher command to rest for a few days and regroup for subsequent missions. But all was not lost. We had the opportunity to improve our performance at NTC and receive a passing score if we could execute the rest of the missions correctly.

My commander at the time, Captain Jason Marc Hancock, a University of Miami graduate who knew how to enjoy life yet was also an Army Ranger and Pathfinder, knew that drastic measures were needed. He told us platoon leaders to wear one piece of civilian clothing from our packing list and meet in his room.

Once we arrived at the commander's room, he looked at me and another lieutenant and instructed us to "commandeer" one of the rental cars from brigade headquarters. I knew this was probably unauthorized, but he was the golden child of the brigade and had direct access to the brigade commander. So, we got the car. The commander then informed us that we were headed for a night out in Las Vegas, which was three hours away!

At that moment, I realized the brilliance of this man and imagined the good times he must have had at the University of Miami while I was slogging away at West Point. He had written out our mission and briefed us in standard military fashion. We were to drive three hours, arriving in Las Vegas by 11:00 p.m., and then enjoy ourselves until 2:30 a.m. We would then drive the three hours back and begin preparations for the next mission at 6:30 a.m. I immediately decided I would drive us to Las Vegas and back because I wanted to maintain control of the situation and, selfishly, keep myself out of military prison or a roadside ditch.

However, a business side to the trip emerged during the three-hour drive. Our executive officer, who was second-in-command and not present at NTC, had personal matters to attend to and had been moved to a new role within the brigade. I thought to myself, *Cool, I'm the junior lieutenant; this doesn't affect me, as I need to continue to lead my platoon.* I was mistaken. Captain Hancock informed me I would assume the role of executive officer from this point forward. I was in shock because typically, the most senior lieutenant is given this role.

Here I was, driving us to Las Vegas to party, with a mission coming up in less than twenty-four hours; I needed to get our command and control in order. The commander told me he had faith in me. As such, I didn't sleep for the next four days, ensuring the command and control were tight and operations were supported from the center. Just like that, I was the executive officer of Charlie Troop, 1st Cavalry. We passed the remainder of the training, and I was even awarded an Army Achievement medal for destroying an enemy reserve. Leaving the training center, I knew I would now have to play a more critical role when the time came to deploy to combat operations. That night in Las Vegas cost me one month's salary, but that's for a different book.

DEPLOYMENT ORDERS

We returned from NTC in August 2002. No sooner had I settled back home than new orders arrived. Another deployment was on the horizon; we were headed to Kuwait in January 2003 to prepare for combat operations. Unlike during the lead-up to Kosovo, I felt more mentally prepared for what lay ahead. The training and previous deployment had taught me a lot about the unpredictability of army life but not necessarily about the dangers that awaited us, especially in a volatile place like Iraq. I knew the risks, but I also understood the importance of staying focused and ready, and I had complete faith in my abilities and experience to guide my next steps.

This deployment was different from the start, but I was glad our unit was prepared to face the challenges ahead. We had bonded well during training and had the right people in the right seats to execute whatever lay ahead. As the executive officer, I departed for Kuwait before the rest of my unit by almost two months. My supply sergeant, Sergeant Jackson, and I had the task of downloading equipment, such as vehicles, weapons, and spare parts, from the port and preparing it for the arrival of Charlie Troop, 1st Cavalry, ensuring all our equipment was accounted for and in place.

Upon arriving in Kuwait, I began executing my tasks immediately. As a leader, I was fully aware of the responsibility on my shoulders. I had to ensure the troops had everything they needed to execute the missions our superior officers assigned to us. I knew my job was far more than handling the logistics; I also had to keep the men focused and manage my commander, who was eager to prove his battlefield prowess. As I mentioned earlier, Captain Hancock graduated from the University of Miami. He could be a frat boy or a serious figure depending on the day and situation.

When I touched down in Kuwait, I was greeted by blistering heat and endless stretches of desert. The air felt thick and dry, with an anticipation that always hung in the background.

I worked with logistics to download the equipment. Sergeant Jackson and I thoroughly inspected everything from vehicles to communication devices to ammunition. We left no stone unturned; everything had to be accounted for. Time passed slowly as I sat in Kuwait counting equipment, keeping a thorough log of everything we would need in combat operations in Iraq.

A couple months later, the rest of the unit arrived. Upon their arrival, I had to double-check each weapon and device they brought, as it would be used by the troops in combat. It was an exhausting and monotonous job; I was bored out of my mind. However, I was fully aware of the serious nature of this check. If Sergeant Jackson or the mechanics had missed anything, it might lead to one of our soldiers losing their life. This burden of responsibility kept me on track and fully motivated.

When the temperature dropped slightly in the evenings, I would sit outside, watching the sun set over the desert. I now had a mental map of everything we would be carrying into combat. Knowing precisely what we had and where it was gave me a sense of control and confidence. It allowed me to visualize our readiness, anticipate our needs, and plan for potential challenges.

COMBAT-READY IN KUWAIT

When I first arrived in Kuwait, I lived in the lap of luxury. I was stationed in Doha, a military base near Kuwait's capital. The area had a strange calmness to it, but beneath the surface, everything was in a state of readiness, and as a military officer, I could sense it. The Doha base was a mix of temporary buildings, supply depots, and vehicles parked in long rows. Sergeant Jackson and I stayed in an air-conditioned trailer, and when I wasn't downloading equipment or preparing troops for combat, I was either lifting weights or playing *NCAA Football 2003*. It is hard to imagine, but I was only twenty-five years old at the time, still a kid.

In February, when the rest of the troops finally arrived, I left Doha and relocated with them to a base camp in the Kuwaiti desert, which the military had named Camp New York. The change was drastic. I had a trailer with air-conditioning and only one roommate in Doha and slept on a mattress. The base camp consisted of nothing more than a collection of tents and temporary structures surrounded by endless stretches of sand. My new bed was a hard military cot in a tent I shared with a dozen snoring soldiers. The cherry on top was the desert's climate, which was extremely harsh: hot during the day, and freezing at night. The wind would kick up sandstorms that made even the simplest tasks difficult. But despite the conditions, we got to work right away. We were given a tight timeline to prepare for combat, so even a day`s delay was impossible.

For a month and a half, we trained intensely in the desert. We would wake up as soon as the sun showed on the horizon and begin the day with physical training and drills. We practiced maneuvers, learned to navigate through desert terrain, and refined our skills in handling weapons, maps, and vehicles. This training was more focused on enhancing our mental toughness. We had to be ready for anything—that was the core objective of the training.

During this time, we also focused on getting the equipment combat-ready, so we kept checking for malfunctions. Then, on March 19, 2003, the official orders were issued by President Bush. We were going to war with Iraq. We had been training for war for quite some time, and that preparation had united us as a unit. When we got the orders to move toward Iraq, we knew we were ready to face whatever came our way. As we packed up and prepared to move out, a sense of purpose settled over us.

CHAPTER 8 TRIGGERS

Reflecting on this time in my life, several moments stand out as potential triggers that may have contributed to my future mental-health challenges. These experiences, while shaping me into a leader and soldier, also left lasting impressions that I continue to reflect on and process.

- One of the first triggers was the abrupt transition from peacekeeping in Kosovo to preparing for combat operations. The emotional conflict I felt upon leaving Kosovo—excitement to return home mixed with sadness for leaving behind the people I had protected—was deeply unsettling. I had grown attached to the resilience of the local people and the sense of purpose I had found in serving them. This emotional tug-of-war left me questioning my ability to detach from the human connections I formed during deployments, a struggle that would resurface in later missions.
- Another significant trigger was the intense pressure and sleep deprivation during the Scout Leaders Course. The relentless pace of eighteen-to-twenty-hour combat simulations followed by minimal

sleep pushed me to my physical and mental limits. The constant fear of failure, knowing that one misstep could send me home, created a lingering sense of anxiety and self-doubt. Even though I succeeded and earned the status of class leader, the toll of operating under such extreme conditions stayed with me, leaving me hyperaware of the consequences of failure in high-stakes situations.

- The spur ride was another moment that tested my resilience. The physical and emotional stress of the twenty-four-hour challenge combined with the taunting and struggle to complete tasks was mentally exhausting. While I persevered and earned my silver spurs, the experience reinforced a pattern of pushing through pain and stress without addressing the emotional impact. This "never quit" mentality, while admirable, may have contributed to a tendency to suppress my feelings and ignore signs of burnout.

- The Mojave Desert training at the NTC introduced a new layer of stress. The repeated failure of our unit against the simulated opposition force was demoralizing. As the newly appointed executive officer, I felt a profound sense of responsibility to address the issues and ensure our success. The sleepless nights spent tightening command and control left me physically drained and emotionally strained. The pressure to perform and the fear of letting my unit down weighed heavily on me, planting seeds of perfectionism and self-imposed responsibility that would later manifest as anxiety.

- The deployment to Kuwait and the preparation for combat in Iraq brought its own set of challenges. The monotony of counting equipment, the harsh desert conditions, and the looming threat of war created a constant undercurrent of stress. The responsibility of inspecting and recording every piece of equipment, knowing that any oversight could cost lives, was overwhelming. The transition from the relative comfort of Doha to the harsh realities of the desert base camp further amplified my mental strain. The relentless training and the knowledge that war was imminent added to the emotional weight I carried.

Each of these moments, while contributing to my growth as a leader, left emotional scars behind. The constant pressure, the physical and mental exhaustion, and the emotional conflicts created a foundation for future struggles with anxiety, stress, and processing traumatic experiences. These triggers, though not immediately apparent, shaped the way I approached challenges and coped with adversity, leaving a lasting impact on my mental health.

CHAPTER 9

UNDER FIRE

AS THE EXECUTIVE OFFICER OF THE BRIGADE RECONNAISsance Troop of the 1st Brigade, 3rd Infantry Division, my job came with immense responsibility. When we were asked to move to Iraq, our brigade commander, Colonel William Grimsley, instructed us to move ahead of the leading ground forces, scout the terrain, clear routes, and provide up-to-the-minute reports about any potential threats or obstacles the troops might encounter on the way.

Essentially, we were the brigade's first line of defense, their eyes and ears on the ground. The success and safety of the entire operation depended on how effectively we gathered and relayed information. We were the spear's tip, and the brigade depended on us to execute.

THE EARLY DAYS OF WAR

Our unit only had a few armored vehicles, and I did not assign myself one. We gave those to the lead scout vehicles, which were likely to engage the enemy first in our battle columns. As scouts, we needed to ensure we could always communicate with the forces behind us; our communications systems enabled us to stay in constant contact with the brigade commander and each other. We had to calculate every movement carefully to prevent fratricide.

The journey from Kuwait to Baghdad, Iraq, was challenging, as we did not know the terrain, dust storms would blow in suddenly and without warning, and we had no idea what the enemy had waiting for us on their turf. We moved from dusty, open stretches of desert into small, scattered towns. The desert was vast and empty, with a harsh sun beating down on us during the day and chilling winds taking over at night. To get a cool drink during the day, we would wrap our sweat-drenched T-shirts around our canteens. The condensation would bring the hot water to a bearable drinking temperature. It felt like drinking warm bath water. The sand also seemed to creep into everything, including our military gear, vehicles, and food. Every breath I took and every meal I ate tasted of dust and rust.

For the first few days after entering Iraq, to our surprise, we encountered little resistance from the Iraqi locals. For the most part, the Iraqis near the Kuwaiti border seemed to be friendly and hospitable by nature. It seemed that many did not even know a war was taking place. In many ways, the initial towns near Kuwait reminded me of Kosovo; we gave kids candy, and people waved as we passed.

We continued to move steadily through town after town, clearing routes and marking safe passages. The lack of engagement was not a source of comfort for me. The soldiers were getting too relaxed and complacent. I had to fight this myself, dozing off from boredom a few times as we made our way deeper into Iraq.

You need to understand that we were not driving at high speeds; it was a slow grind through the desert at fifteen miles per hour. Our main focus at this point was to keep our eyes and ears open. Part of me was happy no one was causing trouble and we had not yet engaged the enemy. But the quiet felt too quiet, like the calm before a storm. Every corner we turned felt dangerous. I tried to encourage the soldiers to always keep their senses on high alert. In a way, I was like a nagging parent to the troops. They were an extension of my family, and I wanted to do everything in my power to protect them.

As we headed north, small groups of locals, mostly children, gathered along the dusty streets. They waved and smiled as our convoy of Humvees passed by, half of which were equipped with mounted .50-caliber machine guns and the other half with Mk 19 automatic grenade launchers. The Mk 19 is a belt-fed weapon that fires 40 mm grenades. Some Iraqis held up peace signs, while others waved makeshift flags or pieces of cloth. Their peaceful attitude was interesting. Seeing our caravan seemed like a moment of excitement for the children in an otherwise difficult life. Some ran alongside the convoy, their laughter cutting through the heavy silence that had followed us for miles. Soldiers in our vehicles tossed out snacks and candy, small gestures that brought broad smiles and grateful hands.

ROUTE BLACK

Calling in a situation report from Iraqi desert

We continued our route toward Baghdad for several days, maintaining constant communication with brigade headquarters. At one point, we were ordered to stop and establish a defensive perimeter as the brigade advanced. Once the administrative team for the brigade was established, the brigade command post was set up at the center of the perimeter. My commander, Captain Hancock, was called to a meeting with the brigade commander and his battalion commanders to discuss battle plans. As he left for the meeting, he handed over command of the troops to me.

It was a typical day in the hot Iraqi desert. The sun was in its full glory, giant in the sky and beating down on us with its relentless heat. Some of the guys were lounging in the shade of the vehicles, checking their gear, while others took a few minutes to rest their eyes. The remainder of the troops were fanned out in hidden positions overlooking the perimeter. Dust hung in the air, and the desert looked empty for miles around. It was a moment of peace during a time of high stress. I decided to make the most of this quiet time with a forty-five-minute power nap. I told Second Lieutenant Michael Hurley, a recent West Point grad, to wake me if he heard from Captain Hancock or we had any action on the perimeter. Twenty minutes into my nap, Second Lieutenant Hurley woke me to tell me Captain Hancock was on his way back. Ten minutes later, Captain Hancock drove up, jumped out of his vehicle, and rushed to my position. He told me to gather the platoon leaders and platoon sergeants in the center of our perimeter. Once we were gathered, we noticed Captain Hancock had created a battle map on the ground. He was holding a big stick in his hand, and he gave us a battle briefing/operations briefing/operations order from the sketches he had drawn in the sand. With his cavalry Stetson on his head and his captain's bars glistening in the sun, he stared at us stoically. It was at this moment that his face went from relaxed to focused. We were now speaking to Billy the Kid, the war fighter.

Captain Hancock's eyes narrowed and his forehead creased. "We've got new orders. Boys, I want you all to pay full attention," he announced over the low chatter of the soldiers around us. His eyes locked onto mine as he added, "We need to clear two routes as quickly as possible—Route Red and Route Black. The brigade is depending on us." A murmur ran through the other leaders in the battle briefing, but Hancock silenced it with a sharp look. "We have intel that Route Red's going to be the hot one. Intelligence reports that contact/direct combat with the enemy is likely. Intelligence reports that Route Black is a bit quieter, but it's still a risky run." He then looked at me and said, "XO, you're taking half the troop down Route Black. I'll handle Route Red. I will take the second platoon with me; I want you to lead the first platoon down Route Black."

I took a deep breath and nodded without hesitation. I respected Hancock; he was always confident, which helped lighten the mood a bit. He would tell the soldiers that we were going to topple Saddam, drink beer, and roast a pig at his palace. He loved taking the toughest jobs that no one else in the troop wanted.

However, unlike Captain Hancock, I was in no hurry to become a hero, get shot, or shoot at others. My focus was on completing the necessary tasks to successfully complete this mission and bring the men back home. I was looking to clear Route Black as quickly and safely as possible. This order, combined with Captain Hancock's passion, was intense, making the war feel real for me. I left the meeting with my orders to brief the troops accompanying me up Route Black; my heart was pounding so hard I thought it would come out of my chest.

I walked over to my men. Soldiers can sense when things are changing, and they were already preparing for whatever came next. "Alright, listen up," I called, clapping my hands to attract their attention. Once I had their full focus, I presented the game plan for the operation, ensuring everyone understood their role in this mission. I looked at each of them then said, "We've got a job to do on Route Black. Let's ensure we conduct weapons checks on the .50-caliber machine guns and the Mk 19 grenade launchers. We must be prepared if something happens. Lock and load your weapons, boys."

I saw Hancock and our first sergeant staring at me, probably wondering why I was rolling out fully loaded. I paused and looked Hancock squarely in his eyes as I said, "Sir, better to be safe than sorry." He nodded and gave a wink, cigar in hand, and began gathering his gear. The soldiers continued their routines in preparation for our movement.

My gunner, Sergeant Ruppe, who was also the unit's chemical sergeant, cracked open every .50-caliber box in the vehicle while my driver, Private

First Class (PFC) Noel Castillo-Reyes, who later retired as a very senior noncommissioned officer, ensured the sight for his weapon was secure. Every one of these troops was laser focused. They wanted to be ready for any surprises. Lives were at stake.

In the background, someone had set up a makeshift sound system. Nothing fancy, just a collection of speakers scavenged from disabled Iraqi vehicles. Troops have a way of making do with whatever they have. When all the equipment was loaded, we were ready to proceed down Route Black. But just before we started moving, one of the guys, Corporal Glover, hit play, and suddenly, 50 Cent's album *Get Rich or Die Trying* blasted through the speakers. The sound echoed over the desert, and the soldiers laughed, if only for a moment. It helped keep our nerves steady.

I then ordered the team to move out, and our convoy roared to life as the engines turned over. We lined up and began heading down Route Black, as ordered. Despite the relative calm, I couldn't shake the feeling that change was coming and would move quickly when it arrived; I felt it in my gut.

CHECKMATE IN SAMAWAH

Sitting in my HMMWV in Iraqi desert, rocket launcher to my back, waiting on next mission

The road ahead was barren, but it held its dangers. We couldn't let our guard down, even though we hadn't encountered much resistance the first few hours, which had been eerily quiet. The soldiers in the vehicles remained vigilant, scanning every building and stretch of road for signs of movement. The .50-caliber and Mk 19 machine gunners kept their eyes peeled, fingers resting lightly on the triggers, ready to react if something went wrong.

We proceeded down Route Black, and for hours, the calm persisted. There was no resistance or signs of danger, so we continued moving. Our intelligence had indicated that the route was clear, but my gut told me otherwise. Everything seemed to be going according to plan: the radio chatter was quiet, and the convoy rolled smoothly. Yet, something felt off. I had learned to trust my instincts in situations like this. The desert was eerily still, and I couldn't shake the feeling that we were being watched.

We passed through a few small towns without any drama, but my instincts kicked in as we approached the larger city of Samawah. I looked at the men and ordered them to have their weapons ready with one round in the chamber, just in case we encountered trouble. I wasn't taking any chances. Compared to the locations we had previously been through, Samawah was significant, and I wanted to stay cautious while passing through a town that size.

We moved through the first half of Samawah without incident. But then, without warning, the lead scout, Staff Sergeant Perkin, came over the radio with a crackling voice: "Contact! Contact!" He was taking fire from the enemy. My heart skipped a beat; things had just gotten serious.

I immediately shouted into the hand microphone to engage the enemy. The Humvee jolted as the .50-caliber gunner opened fire, the rounds exploding in the air with deafening power. Heavy brass shells dropped onto the vehicle's floor. I grabbed the handheld microphone and informed brigade headquarters that we were in an intense firefight. Our attached Combat Observation and Lasing Team (COLT) platoon leader began lasing targets and directing artillery fire. Meanwhile, my scouts continued to engage the enemy, unleashing a barrage of firepower against them. My adrenaline was pumping, but I had to stay focused on the present and consider our next move. We were now engaged in a deadly game of chess.

My driver, PFC Castillo-Reyes, was doing his best to maneuver the vehicle while also firing his M4 out the window as if he were in a drive-by shooting. I snapped at him, "Focus on driving this truck, bro!" I could not afford to have a distracted driver, especially when we were in the midst of a firefight and the terrain and enemy were unfamiliar.

Amid all the chaos, something unusual caught my attention: The enemy was retreating despite being the superior force. I wondered, *Why are they falling back now?* We were only a platoon and a half of scouts. While we were relentless, I knew we lacked the firepower to force any enemy into submission. In that moment, I recalled my training from the Scout Leaders Course, which emphasized understanding the terrain, assessing the situation, and identifying the missing link.

As I stared at my map, I realized what was happening: We were heading straight for a small bridge. The enemy was directing us there because it would be their kill zone. By simulating retreat, they were attempting to herd us toward the bridge, likely planning to blow it—and us—up once we were on it. I thought to myself, *This is a strategy I would certainly use.*

I could not risk my men ending up on that bridge, so I acted quickly. I grabbed the hand microphone and shouted into the radio, "Turn around and reorient your fire to the buildings; we are fighting our way out!" They were surprised, but there was not enough time to explain. The troops quickly adjusted their positions, and we fought our way back out of Samawah.

Bullets zipped past as we maneuvered our way out, but we increased the pressure, returning fire while continuing to identify artillery targets. After some time, we successfully exited the town, established a perimeter, and took a secure overwatch position oriented toward Samawah, maintaining that position until our brigade's main element arrived. One thing was clear: We had outsmarted them—checkmate! I looked at the faces of my men and could see this battle had sharpened our awareness, especially considering we had lived to fight another day.

We sat in the overwatch position on the outskirts of Samawah for about an hour, recording the grid coordinates of the targets we had identified. The radio was quiet for a bit as the main element made its approach, and the dust from the battle began to settle. Adrenaline still coursed through my veins, but the tension in the air had eased slightly. We had fought our way through, and now, we waited to see if higher command wanted us to reengage the enemy in the town.

As I glanced at my soldiers and ensured they were being treated for their injuries, I noticed many were quietly lost in thought. This was the first of many battles to come. We learned from this encounter that the bonds we had forged would help us in the heat of battle. These men, whom I affectionately called my brothers, had my back when it mattered most, and I had theirs.

There had been no hesitation in their movements, no second-guessing when I ordered them to engage. They had responded without question, trusting one another in ways that could only have been forged through their physical fitness training, the spur ride, and combat training at the NTC, all of which they had undertaken together.

I watched as one of the younger soldiers wiped the sweat from his brow, his hands still shaking a little—not from fear, but from the intensity of what we had just experienced. Another, more-experienced soldier, Staff Sergeant Aaron Davis, sat back and leaned his head against the wall, eyes scanning the area, constantly alert. Yet, even in his calm demeanor, I could see a glint of respect and gratitude in his eyes: He understood we had just navigated through something dangerous that could have ended very differently.

I turned my gaze to the rest of the troops. Each of them was doing what needed to be done—checking weapons, maintaining their vehicles, and staying vigilant. But I knew, deep down, we all felt the same thing: a deep, unspoken awareness that we had just faced something as a unit and emerged on the other side together. That kind of bond doesn't happen overnight. We had become a family, and in the chaos of war, that connection is more valuable than anything else.

As I pondered these ideas, the radio crackled to life with a message from Colonel Grimsley, the brigade commander. He conveyed the next set of orders in his distinctive voice: I was to take my scouts around the town and rejoin Route Black to investigate the area further. I responded, "Roger, sir," and instructed my troops to move up the route.

As we moved up the route, I grabbed a pack of cigarettes, opened it, and started smoking. I had never smoked before, but the pressure of the moment pushed me to do it. My mind was racing, and I wasn't accustomed to this kind of chaos. Shots were being fired, grenades were exploding, cars were being damaged, and people were running in every direction. The tumult around me was unbelievable. Lighting a cigarette felt like the only way to calm my nerves. Before I realized it, I had smoked an entire pack in just an hour.

Samawah wasn't just any battle: It was my first taste of combat, and it was intense. That town is forever etched into my memory and spirit. It was the first of many battles I would face and served as a wake-up call. I realized this deployment was a dire life-or-death situation and understood that things could get considerably tougher.

Once we advanced along Route Black toward Baghdad, Samawah was no longer in our control. The main force had taken over the fight, and it would take them several more days to finally capture the city.

Despite the relentless stress of combat during our march to Baghdad and subsequent missions, I focused on the tasks assigned by our commanders. I led my scouts, trusting that the bond we shared would help us through whatever challenges we encountered. The road ahead would be long and uncertain, but we were prepared. Most importantly, we were in it together. That was what mattered most.

THE BOND OF BROTHERHOOD

The soldiers of Charlie Troop, 1st Cavalry, epitomized team spirit and family. Like any family, we experienced infighting at times, but we overcame those challenges, and I continue to support my comrades in every way I can. The members of Charlie Troop exemplified the true meanings of unity and resilience, standing together through thick and thin and embodying an unwavering spirit of camaraderie and commitment in the face of the harsh realities of war.

My time in Iraq broadened my perspectives on humanity and mortality. I did not see the individuals we were fighting against as enemies filled with hatred. Rather, I recognized them as people much like myself, dedicated to their cause and willing to sacrifice their lives if necessary. While I disagreed with their ideology, I understood what motivated them and why they were fighting. They were victims of circumstance more than cartoon villains filled with nothing but evil and malice. Though I didn't relish fighting these people, I knew what I had signed up for when I joined the United States Army, and I felt it was important to honor the oath I took.

After each skirmish ended and the smoke cleared, I felt a mix of emotions. I was relieved my soldiers and I had survived, but I also mourned any young lives lost too soon. The complexities of war, along with my reflections on mortality and humanity, left a lasting impact on me. These experiences can lead to various consequences, including PTSD.

The emotional toll of witnessing the sacrifices and losses of war, coupled with the internal conflict of understanding and grappling with its realities, can contribute to the psychological challenges faced by many veterans. These internal struggles, often hidden beneath layers of resilience and duty, reveal the profound and enduring effects of war on the human psyche and the journey veterans must take toward healing and understanding. At the time, I was unaware my journey with mental health was about to begin.

CHARLIE TROOP IN BAGHDAD

Re-creating the comforts of home at Hancock's Outpost

Hancock's Outpost on the outskirts of Baghdad

I could easily write an entire book about the adventures of Charlie Troop, 1st Cavalry, on our trek to Baghdad. Once there, we were among the first to occupy Saddam's palaces in the city, where we cleared out the buildings for the eventual construction of the Green Zone. We also participated in clearing Baghdad International Airport.

As a brigade asset, battalion commanders often sought permission from the brigade to send us out on unorthodox missions. For instance, Staff Sergeant Aaron Davis was assigned to guard a major bridge with only four combat Humvees and air defense artillerymen in Bradleys who were not necessarily trained for ground combat. Despite the challenges, our team always made it back home because we consistently found ways to survive.

Once the Green Zone was secured, we were ordered to conduct missions across Baghdad from an old, abandoned high-rise. While it wasn't glamorous, that high-rise had electricity. Sitting in the building, our unit was bored, but we were much more comfortable sleeping on deserted Iraqi beds than the desert floor. Many of the guys, including me, had gone almost two months without a shower during our push to Baghdad. While I didn't exactly enjoy being bored, I would never complain about being comfortable. Additionally, it gave me time to write letters to my family, relax in an air-conditioned room, and enjoy something other than warm water to drink.

However, after a couple weeks in that high-rise, my commander, Captain Hancock, somehow convinced the brigade that his unit needed to move to a random outpost. He was no longer satisfied with being bored and comfortable; he wanted to get out and establish his missions, capture contraband, and engage with the locals on his terms. Additionally, I am sure he did not appreciate being under the deputy brigade commander's thumb.

On one hand, I didn't want to leave, but on the other, boredom was starting to set in. The troop had begun taking unnecessary risks, like going downtown to order buckets of fried chicken or visiting "Pizza Hot" (yes, "Hot," not "Hut") to buy pizza made with goat cheese. Of note: Combat soldiers will eat anything when they are bored and hungry. The soldiers of 1st Brigade, 3rd Infantry Division, were purchasing so much food, cigarettes, and soda that the street merchants realized the brown-skinned soldiers preferred grape and orange soda, while the white soldiers favored Coke and Pepsi. They began to market their products accordingly, including bootleg movies and music.

Our next move took us to an old house on the outskirts of Baghdad. The house lacked windows, electricity, and basic comforts. Captain Hancock and one of the platoons had previously used it as a stopover on their way to Baghdad, and the commander had noted it as a potential site for an outpost. Since this house had been the site of a recent battle, it also had no air-conditioning, running water, or functioning utilities. The only positive aspect of the house was that it helped refocus the troops on our mission and removed us from the oversight of high command. Additionally, it provided an excellent setting for some very interesting and animated games of spades.

After a month at Captain Hancock's outpost, the commander received new military orders and returned to the United States. Before he left, the brigade held a ceremony for Captain Hancock and me to present us with our Bronze Stars and valor devices for actions taken in combat. A week later, I was promoted to captain, removed from Charlie Troop, and reassigned to the brigade administrative staff. I was sent to an infantry battalion to serve as the battalion adjutant, replacing the former adjutant while he returned to the States due to significant family issues. Shortly thereafter, I took over as the full-time adjutant. Charlie Troop now had a new leadership team, marking the end of my journey serving with those great men.

THE DELIVERY GUY

Transitioning to the role of adjutant in an infantry battalion came with its own set of challenges. First, I was not an Infantry officer; I was an Armor officer. However, the battalion needed an officer who could follow orders and get things done. Given that we were at war, the assignment officials did not believe my branch mattered, so off I went to be an infantry adjutant.

My core responsibilities as a battalion adjutant were supposed to focus on administrative tasks, such as managing personnel records, handling human resources functions, ensuring that soldiers received awards for their service, processing promotions, and designing flight manifests for those returning stateside. In theory, this role should have kept me behind a desk in an air-conditioned office.

However, having just come from the brigade scouts, I was assigned the additional task of delivering hot meals to infantry units stationed at outposts outside the secure zone. I couldn't believe it—after surviving numerous skirmishes as a scout, my reward was to risk my life delivering hot meals and mail and allowing soldiers to use my satellite phone or send emails. Essentially, I became a combat version of Uber Eats, equipped with a free satellite phone and internet capabilities. I had come full circle from my days as a paperboy.

While none of these deliveries turned into firefights like those I experienced as a scout, we were shot at several times. Every time I went out on a delivery, my stress level was high, and I ensured my crew remained alert, as becoming too relaxed could put lives at risk.

Once the orders for exit arrived, one of my responsibilities was to create the flight manifests for everyone in my brigade to leave Iraq. Coordinating these flight manifests was a significant task, as they were necessary for thousands of soldiers to depart the country in an orderly fashion. This role meant I would be among the last soldiers to head home. This situation tested my resolve; I had been one of the first to arrive, and now, I would be one of the last to leave. However, that was part of the job, so I set my emotions aside and focused on executing my duties.

LESSONS LEARNED FROM IRAQ

My experiences in Iraq instilled in me a deep appreciation for the small things in life, a lesson for which I am truly grateful. They taught me to value the United States' comforts and strengthened my understanding of teamwork and sacrifice.

Wars have a way of revealing aspects of people they may not even be aware of. Poets and authors have written extensively about war and the lessons it imparts to humanity. Emotions run high during conflicts, and the fear of death becomes an ever-present companion, like a heartbeat, always with you.

This unique pressure pushes you to reach beyond your limits. In war, every action could be your last, keeping you alert and on your toes. Your senses are heightened to the point where you anticipate every potential danger at the slightest sound or detail. It's mentally and physically exhausting, but soldiers must keep pushing forward—for themselves and those around them.

One important lesson I learned is that everyone handles war differently. People's reactions to stress and fear can be surprising. Soldiers who seemed rugged and unbreakable during training might freeze or shut down when confronted with the chaos of actual combat. The bravado they displayed in safe environments can vanish in an instant. Conversely, quiet and unassuming individuals, whom you might not expect to thrive in such conditions, can step up in awe-inspiring ways, becoming the rock-solid teammates you can rely on when it truly matters.

I have witnessed soldiers confront their fears boldly, even when the odds were against them. Some used humor to lighten the mood, shielding themselves from the gravity of the situation; at times, this approach was effective, while at other times, it was not. Others focused intently on the task, channeling their energy into staying sharp and making it through another day. Some leaned on their faith in God or connections with their comrades, drawing strength from the bonds formed with their brothers and sisters in arms.

War changes how you see yourself. It strips away the facades, laying bare your true nature. In the face of death, you're forced to confront your strengths and weaknesses. You might unearth depths of courage you never knew you had or be humbled by your own limits. These moments define you, shaping who you are. You may emerge from the crucible stronger or weaker, forever marked by the trials of combat.

When asked about my experiences during the war, I acknowledge I faced numerous challenges, particularly when it came to making life-or-death decisions. I found that keeping the reality of death and combat at the forefront of my mind enabled me to adopt a "them or me" mentality. It eliminated gray areas for me. I held the belief that if I didn't strike my enemy first, they would try to kill me. This belief became foundational in how I operated and was a message I instilled in the soldiers under my command. While survival was never guaranteed, maintaining a clear focus kept us sharp and prepared.

THE HARSH REALITIES OF COMBAT

The men of Charlie Troop, 1st Cavalry, never sought out combat; none of us wanted to engage in a firefight or risk our lives without reason. However, when the fight came, we responded with everything we had. There was no room for half measures or second-guessing. We fought fiercely, not out of anger but from a profound will to survive and protect one another. Every soldier knew their life depended on the person next to them. During this time, my senses were constantly on high alert, and when I returned home from Iraq, the severe headaches I had faced years earlier at West Point returned.

When I got back to the United States, I put on a facade of confidence and made it seem like my deployment to Iraq had been a breeze. However, I constantly felt uneasy, had trouble sleeping, and endured nightmares. One incident from my deployment has haunted me since it happened. Parts of my unit and I were deep in the desert, enduring the scorching heat as we tried to navigate past a known minefield. We stopped to read the map and find our bearings in front of my Humvee. Unfortunately, a soldier inadvertently singled me out as the leader at that moment, signaling to the enemy who was in charge.

Later that day, I was in the same area, using the rearview mirror of my Humvee to shave. I was carefully dragging the razor across my face when suddenly, in what felt like a miraculous moment, the razor, as if slapped by my guardian angel, flew from my hand, landing in the sand below. As I bent down to pick it up, a sharp crack pierced the air, and the mirror I had been looking into shattered into jagged pieces. The bullet missed me. However, in my nightmares, the bullet hits me every time, and I see my friends and family gathered around me at my funeral.

Instances like this contributed to my PTSD diagnosis. Being a warrior and overseeing others was more than just a job; it was a heavy weight on my shoulders, a burden my soul had to carry that filled me with constant worry. I was responsible for the lives of many. The soldiers under my command were not just names or ranks; they were real people with families, dreams, and futures. Every decision I made was crucial, and I was always aware that my choices could impact the lives and loved ones of everyone around me. This was the burden I carried daily. The thought of letting them down or failing in my duty was terrifying, especially knowing that we all had family back home depending on us to make it back.

CHAPTER 9 TRIGGERS

During my time in Iraq, I encountered several intense situations that triggered mental-health issues, contributing to my future struggles. As the executive officer of the Brigade Reconnaissance Troop, my role came with immense responsibility, and the pressure was relentless.

- One of the most significant triggers was the constant fear of the unknown. The journey from Kuwait to Baghdad was fraught with uncertainty, marked by dust storms, unfamiliar terrain, and potential enemy threats. This constant state of alertness and the need to be prepared for any situation took a toll on my mental health.
- Another major trigger was the intense firefight in Samawah. When Staff Sergeant Perkin's voice crackled over the radio, announcing contact with the enemy, my heart skipped a beat. The adrenaline rush and chaos of the battle were overwhelming. My driver, PFC Castillo-Reyes, was firing his M4 out the window while trying to maneuver the vehicle, and I had to snap at him to focus on driving. The enemy's retreat, despite being the superior force, added to the confusion and stress. The chilling realization that we were being herded toward a kill zone at the bridge was shocking. The quick decision to turn around and fight our way out of Samawah was desperate, and the bullets zipping past us as we maneuvered out added to the trauma.

- The aftermath of the battle was another significant trigger. The sight of my soldiers lost in thought and the awareness that this was just the beginning of many battles weighed heavily on me. The bond we had forged was crucial, but the emotional toll of witnessing sacrifices and losses was immense. The internal conflict of grappling with the realities of war contributed to the psychological challenges I faced.
- One incident that haunts me was the day we attempted to navigate past a known minefield. A soldier inadvertently singled me out as the leader, indicating to the enemy who was in charge. Later, while shaving using the rearview mirror of my Humvee, a bullet shattered the mirror, narrowly missing me. This incident played repeatedly in my mind, contributing to my PTSD diagnosis.

These triggers, combined with the constant worry and responsibility for the lives of my soldiers, created a heavy burden on my soul. The thought of letting them down or failing in my duty was terrifying, especially knowing we all had family back home depending on us to make it back. My experiences in Iraq were pivotal in shaping my mental-health struggles and contributed to the issues I faced in the future.

Part III

BATTLING ON THE HOME FRONT

CHAPTER 10

HOW DID I GET HERE?

WHEN I RETURNED FROM IRAQ, I WAS NOT THE SAME PERSON: I had changed dramatically. I had become a nervous man, constantly on edge. Every loud sound or sudden movement drew my attention to my new reality. I could no longer sit with my back to the door at restaurants; I always had to see who was coming in and out of the room. Additionally, my head pounded, and my voice would sometimes waver unexpectedly.

Before I went to Iraq, my closest friends would have described me as the life of the party—confident and outgoing. I was never someone who thought about my mortality or withdrew from society. However, after I returned home, my friends noticed a significant change in me. They observed that I had become more withdrawn and prone to sudden outbursts of anger. I used to love debating, but after coming back, I lost interest in lively discussions and would often leave the room or avoid conversations altogether.

They remarked on my hypervigilance, as I constantly scanned my surroundings for threats, even in safe environments. They noticed I had a tendency to not show up to social gatherings. When I did attend, I would isolate myself and struggle to connect with people outside my trusted circle. They also commented on my increased aggression; once I set my mind on something, I felt compelled to obtain it.

In many ways, I never left that desert; I am always waiting for the unexpected. It is exhausting, and I know I will have to deal with this for the rest of my life.

ESCAPING THROUGH FRIENDSHIP

A way to cope with old friends who comment on how much you've changed—and avoid dealing with your issues—is to meet new friends who accept you as you are. An additional coping mechanism is alcohol. Prior to going to Iraq, I probably had one drink a month. That changed to a few drinks a day.

Two weeks after I returned to American soil, I ran into fellow officers Pete Frometta, Shawn Gines, and Walter Pridgen at the post finance office. We were all there for the same reason: to sort out the chaotic finances of our soldiers who had struggled to manage their funds during deployment.

From the moment we connected, it was clear we had a lot in common, which allowed our friendship to develop quickly. Pete, who is Dominican, radiates infectious energy, while Shawn, who is Puerto Rican and Italian, brings a laid-back charm to every situation. Walter, who is African American, was the glue that brought us all together. All three of them grew up in New York City, and together, we formed a vibrant circle of friends in Savannah, Georgia, eager to enjoy life after deployment.

Our primary goal was simple: enjoy life to the fullest. Every weekend—sometimes even on weekdays—we would hop on our motorcycles and feel the wind whip past us as we rode down winding roads. With my newfound love for liquor, I no longer had an issue being social. My friends and I often hit up bars, reveling in the camaraderie and laughter that filled the air. Our nights were long, frequently stretching into the early hours of the morning. If there was an event, party, get-together, or any gathering that seemed even slightly interesting, we would be there. It got to the point where I carried a backpack filled with bottles of alcohol everywhere we went. Additionally, I carried white rum in a water bottle to help take the edge off and make mingling easier.

At the time, I didn't fully grasp the impact of my actions. My work performance remained unaffected; I could still run two miles in under twelve minutes and complete over one hundred push-ups and sit-ups in two minutes, scoring perfectly on the fitness test. Despite my unhealthy habits, I remained fit and continued to make significant contributions at work. Looking back now, it's obvious that my whirlwind of activity and drinking were coping mechanisms—ways to drown out the haunting memories and stresses from my leadership experiences in Iraq, as well as other lingering worries in my mind.

Being surrounded by peers who had faced similar harrowing experiences provided a sense of comfort. However, deep down, I was merely avoiding the fear, guilt, and vivid memories that plagued me. Instead of confronting the emotional aftermath of my deployment, I buried it beneath layers of noise, liquor, and constant activity, hoping that, eventually, those feelings would subside or fade away.

DEALING WITH THE SYMPTOMS

Eventually, the 24/7 lifestyle began to take a toll on me. One cold winter night, I was feeling significantly under the weather. However, it was Tuesday, a major party night in Savannah, and Pete, Shawn, Walter, and the guys had plans to go to a club. I told Pete I was feeling ill, but being Dominican, he had a concoction for my sickness that, in hindsight, was probably just Brugal Rum, honey, and some lemon juice. I drank the concoction, slowly got dressed, and headed out with the guys. Throughout the night, I sipped on Pete's "medicine," and honestly, I felt pretty good. The night ended around 3:00 a.m., and when I got home, I passed out.

The next day, I didn't wake up until 11:00 a.m., despite being scheduled to be at work by 6:00 a.m. I soon realized I was too weak to get out of bed. Luckily, my cell phone was nearby, so I called the hospital and arranged for an ambulance to come and pick me up. The ambulance rushed me to the hospital, where doctors ran a series of tests and quickly diagnosed me with pneumonia. My immune system had finally caught up with me, issuing a stern warning: I was pushing my health too far.

At the hospital, the doctors immediately started me on medication, administering strong antibiotics through an IV and giving me something to help ease my breathing. The hospital staff monitored me closely, and I spent the next week confined to a hospital bed. It was a lonely but much-needed experience. Along with plenty of sleep, I had abundant time to reflect on how my choices had led me there, and I continuously pondered how my life could return to normal. One thing became clear: My decisions were a result of my experiences in Iraq and the PTSD that seemed to have become a part of me.

Even after the pneumonia was gone, my lungs did not feel the same. That week in the hospital was a turning point, making me realize I could not continue living as I had. My body was not invincible, and I had to slow down my drinking. The partying and other reckless behaviors had been my way of coping, but I couldn't keep running forever. I knew I was headed for rock bottom, but I wasn't there just yet. I was more focused on treating the symptoms than eliminating the causes of my issues.

There were numerous signs of PTSD that I had continued to ignore. I often found myself gasping for breath in my car, feeling like the world was closing in on me. While driving, I would grip the steering wheel tightly, and anxiety would hit me out of nowhere. Sometimes, I felt like I couldn't breathe and had to pull over to catch my breath. Most of the time, however, I kept driving aimlessly, as if I could outrun the chaos in my mind.

STRUGGLES OF THE MIND

In addition to my breathing struggles, I was also battling paranoia. I thought that everyone was out to get me. This belief was a fleeting thought and a conviction that ran deep within me. Whether at work or in my personal life, I always felt like people were trying to sabotage me, ruin my career, or hurt me. I had become suspicious of everyone, building walls around myself to preemptively shut people out before they could cause me harm.

Living this way made it impossible to trust anyone. I was constantly bracing myself for betrayal or disappointment. Even when people were genuine and kind, I struggled to interpret their actions positively. Instead, I viewed their behavior through a lens of suspicion, constantly second-guessing their true intentions. Over time, this distrust infiltrated every relationship—whether with friends, colleagues, or loved ones. I couldn't let my guard down, fearing they would ultimately let me down or try to hurt me.

I also battled with my temper, which I had no control over. I could go from calm and friendly to completely enraged in seconds without any real reason. The most minor incidents, like someone cutting me off in traffic or making an offhand comment, would set me off. My anger would explode, leaving me feeling drained and ashamed. Over time, I recognized how my outbursts harmed my relationships, yet I felt powerless to manage my emotions.

This anger hurt the people around me the most. I pushed friends away, lost relationships, and alienated those who cared about me. They did not understand why I was always angry, and I was unable to explain it. I was so wrapped up in my pain and fear that I could not see how my behavior was tearing everything apart.

Images of the pain, suffering, and death I had witnessed in Iraq replayed endlessly in my mind. The violence, bloodshed, and loss of life on both sides were impossible to forget, not to mention the stress. I could not go a day without thinking about them, and it wore me down.

I would wake up in the middle of the night, heart racing and gasping for air, convinced death had come for me in the darkness. I could not explain it to anyone, not even my closest friends. It felt like I was trapped in my mind. My brain could not differentiate between what had happened in the past and what was happening in the present; I was hyperaware of my issues.

WAR IS CHAOS

In movies, war is often portrayed through the eyes of the leading characters, who are often depicted as mythical heroes. The battles happen, and you see the supporting cast and extras dying or being injured, but if the main characters are okay, it's not a problem. The rest of the folks just don't matter. Everything appears to be under control, as though there is a plan that everything follows.

I grew up thinking war was interesting, but thanks to recent war documentaries, I now understand it is anything but glamorous. Politicians who have never experienced combat often discuss military action as if the

United States can simply enter a country, engage in a few battles, and take control with little to no resistance. However, we know that when people are determined to fight, they will respond fiercely, regardless of how outmanned or outgunned they are. This leads to a tragic series of funerals, marking the moment we realize that war is grueling, exhausting, and chaotic.

Movies don't show the long periods soldiers endure when they can't clean and care for themselves. There were months we did not have access to showers, and basic hygiene became an afterthought. We wore the same clothes day after day covered in dust, sweat, and grime. We learned to live with the smell because there was little we could do about it.

The equipment does not always function the way it does in the movies, either. Guns jam, radios fail, and even the simplest tasks can become struggles. We had to make do with what we had, often improvising and fixing things ourselves when supplies were low or our equipment broke down.

A few months after I returned home from the hospital and had fully recovered from pneumonia, I received new orders. The army was sending me back to West Point to work in the Office of Admissions as a recruiter. My time in the 3rd Infantry Division had come to an end. I was sad, but I took pride in knowing I would be helping shape the future of the army by returning to West Point and contributing to the development of the next generation of selfless leaders. I hoped leaving Fort Stewart would be the change I needed to get my life in order. I thought to myself, *Maybe this will help me overcome the jump starts and scares that I've been experiencing occasionally. Maybe this is what I need*, unaware that something significant was waiting for me that would make my current battle with PTSD seem small by comparison.

BACK ON THE HUDSON

Now back at West Point and serving in the Office of Admissions, I felt like I was at a turning point. This role provided a vital new mission in my life and truly reenergized me. The day I received the orders to return to West Point marked one of the happiest I had experienced in a long time. I was excited to begin a new chapter that would bring a glimmer of hope back into my life.

My mission as an admissions officer was clear: We sought talented and qualified candidates from diverse backgrounds to join West Point. While this role differed significantly from traditional combat or peacekeeping missions, it had its own meaningful purpose. I was grateful to be engaged in something productive and positive that helped distract me from the negative thoughts and painful memories lingering in my mind.

Although this new assignment wasn't physically demanding, I must admit that earning a spot on this team was no small feat. To be selected as an admissions officer, candidates needed an exceptional military career that demonstrated skill, discipline, leadership, and resilience. As I mentioned before, I was a functioning alcoholic who managed to excel at work despite my struggles off the clock. The application process was tedious and rigorous, requiring a detailed and flawless submission that left no room for doubt. I was ecstatic when my application was selected, giving me the chance to contribute to building the diversity of two classes at West Point. It was a worthwhile mission. Being part of this team was more than just a new job or assignment; it felt like a fresh start. It enhanced my public speaking skills and reignited my academic interests.

Additionally, the admissions office had clear purposes and priorities—something I desperately needed after the chaos and uncertainty I had experienced. My days were no longer empty or burdened by the past; they were filled with meaningful work, connection, and the concrete goal of building a bridge between West Point and the diverse communities we envisioned the next generation of army officers representing.

In my role as an admissions officer, I had the opportunity to speak about West Point and its service at various venues. In the Deep South, many high schools would gather their entire student body to hear my presentations. I never limited my talking points solely to West Point; instead, I emphasized the endless opportunities available to all students, regardless of their race, gender, or ethnicity, if they applied their unique talents. I also spoke at churches, visited candidates' homes to talk with their parents, and even had the chance to present at congressional events. The details really mattered in this job, and it helped me curb my drinking habits since my colleagues and superiors were highly skilled individuals who would quickly notice and call out any bad habits.

HAUNTED BY HEADACHES

A few months passed smoothly as I enjoyed every moment of my new role in the Office of Admissions. Life finally seemed to be settling into a rhythm. I loved my work; it felt like my true purpose in life. I experienced a sense of pride every day knowing that I was productive and positively impacting the lives of others. However, out of nowhere, an old and unwelcome visitor reappeared in my life: the debilitating headaches I used to experience while playing football.

I still remember the first wave of excruciating pain hitting me on a crisp fall morning while I was in my office reviewing candidate applications. It came out of nowhere. As I was sipping my coffee, a sharp, pounding pain suddenly took hold of my head. I initially tried closing my eyes to give them a rest, but this was not the average headache most people experience from time to time. It felt as if someone was squeezing my skull from the inside.

The pain was so intense I wouldn't wish it on my worst enemy. It lasted a long time, and I ended up turning off the lights in my shared office and curling up under my desk, praying the headache would subside. My office mate and West Point classmate John Thurman (now Dr. John Thurman), found me under the desk and helped me get home. At that time, he was also my next-door neighbor. As I lay on my bed after taking a few Excedrin, I wondered how and why the headache had occurred. It brought back memories I had hoped to leave behind.

This headache was twice as bad as the ones I had experienced on the practice field at West Point. Back then, I couldn't tell whether they were caused by the brutal nature of the game, pressure to compete while trying to avoid injury, relentless training combined with long nights of studying, or adrenaline that masked everything else when the violent hits happened. I always believed the headaches were just a normal part of the sport—something to endure. They also did not render me completely immobilized, as this new version did.

But now, years later and far removed from the field, the pain had returned twice as bad, and I couldn't use those same excuses to ease my racing heartbeat. Each day after a headache, I returned to work to keep myself occupied. I even continued to travel several times a month. However, in the back of my mind, I constantly feared that the headache would return. I took headache medication everywhere I went as a precautionary measure. If I even felt a slight pain, I would immediately take a pain reliever.

I came up with all kinds of reasons for my headaches. I told myself it was just stress, dehydration, or perhaps caffeine withdrawal. I invented myriad excuses and tried to brush them off. However, they did not stop. They became more frequent, each one hitting harder and lasting longer.

Some days, I would be in the middle of an important meeting or a conversation with a potential recruit when I would feel that familiar throbbing creeping in. I would pop painkillers from my desk drawer, but that only dulled the pain's intensity; they never fully stopped it. The only cure was a dark room and sleep.

SELF-ADVOCACY

Around the same time that the headaches reoccurred, another issue began to trouble me. Over the past few years, I had noticed that my voice would sometimes become hoarse for no apparent reason. It wasn't constant, but the hoarseness would come and go. At times, I could not speak entirely, almost as if my vocal cords were playing a cruel game of hide-and-seek.

Speaking was a significant part of my job, so the hoarseness made me self-conscious. During presentations, my voice would suddenly fade, leaving me breathless. I learned to disguise it as an intelligent pause, using the opportunity to sip water before continuing.

It was frustrating and embarrassing, but I couldn't determine its cause. I made several hospital appointments to discuss my headaches and hoarse voice. The headaches led to my being prescribed numerous painkillers, whereas the hoarseness had no real cure. The doctors and nurses recommended I gargle salt water every day, but obviously, that did nothing.

After a terrible headache one afternoon, I decided not to ignore them any longer, and I went to the emergency room at Keller Army Community Hospital at West Point. The doctor was thorough with his checkup; the initial assessment did not reveal anything concerning, which was a relief. The doctor also ran a few basic tests and told me everything seemed normal. I came home relieved, but something did not sit right with me. I knew these were not just random headaches or minor issues with my voice. These felt connected in some way, and I knew they would eventually return. I felt like I was on the clock, but I did not know for what.

The same weekend as my doctor's visit, I went to see a friend in Washington, DC. This friend, Roger Mack, was a professional track athlete and is now a renowned fitness trainer who owns Optimum Sports and Fitness in the DC area. Roger invited me to work out at his facility, and while I was doing overhead lifts, he noticed my left trapezius muscle was significantly smaller than my right one. He suggested I might be experiencing muscle atrophy. This information was crucial for me. Armed with Roger's assessment, I returned to the hospital a few days later after experiencing another episode of severe headaches. I explained my history with these headaches, detailing how they had started when I was playing football and had now returned with a vengeance.

I also described the hoarseness I had been experiencing, emphasizing its duration and impact on my life. Additionally, I mentioned the atrophy in my trapezius muscle. Despite my concerns, the doctor was about to send me home with more medications. However, this time, I strongly advocated for myself.

Eventually, I convinced the doctor to schedule a magnetic resonance imaging (MRI) examination and a computed tomography (CT) scan. The doctor picked up on my concern and obliged my request for the imaging tests. I felt relieved that someone was finally taking me seriously, but I also experienced a wave of anxiety. A CT scan meant we were probing deeper, both literally and figuratively. Part of me wanted answers, but another part of me feared what we might find.

This experience reinforced for me the importance of advocating for one's own health. It's crucial to speak up about your concerns and ensure your voice is heard in the healthcare system. Trusting your instincts and pushing for the tests or treatments you think are necessary can make all the difference in getting the care you deserve. Remember, you are your own best advocate when navigating your health journey.

Another important issue I want to address is hospital anxiety, which particularly affects men, especially veterans and Black and Hispanic men. This anxiety often prevents them from attending scheduled checkups and advocating for their health. We need to tackle this problem, as it could help save countless lives and prevent more serious health issues in the future.

THE GOLF BALL IN MY HEAD

Doctor's assessment before surgery

MEDICAL RECORD	CHRONOLOGICAL RECORD OF MEDICAL CARE	AUTHORIZED FOR LOCAL REPRODUCTION
DATE	SYMPTOMS, DIAGNOSIS, TREATMENT, TREATING ORGANIZATION *(Sign each entry)*	

6/10/05
1400

Counseling Note:

The risks, benefits and alternatives of resection of jugular bulb tumor were discussed. The risks include but are not limited to: bleeding, pain, hypothesia, infection, changes in smell and/or taste, facial nerve dysfunction with paresis or paralysis, CSF leak, scarring, headaches, cosmetic deformity residual/recurrent tumor, need for further surgery, change in voice/swallowing, need for trach/feeding tube, shoulder weakness, persistent hearing loss, complete hearing loss, vertigo, loss of hair, seizures, risk of anesthesia and other medications, undesired cosmetic result, injury to other nerves and vessels, injury to the dura/brain, injury to other surrounding structures, temporary and permanent disability, and death. Patient and/or guardian(s) state understanding of these risks and desire to proceed.

Brian J. McKinnon, MD
CDR, MC, USN
Neurotology/Otology

CHRONOLOGICAL RECORD OF MEDICAL CARE
Medical Record
STANDARD FORM 600 (REV. 6-97)
Prescribed by GSA/ICMR
FIRMR (41 CFR) 201-9.202-1

Doctor's assessment before surgery

A few days after the CT scan, my phone rang at work. It was the doctor from Keller Hospital. He asked me to come back to the hospital to review my scans. I could tell by his tone that something was wrong, which made my heart skip a beat; I could feel it in my stomach.

When I arrived, the doctor led me into his office and asked me to sit down. "We found something on the scan," he said, carefully weighing his words. "You have a brain tumor about the size of a golf ball, and it's pressing against critical nerves; I recommend you have surgery immediately."

For a moment, my world came to a standstill. I stared at him, struggling to process his words. A brain tumor? Surgery? How could this be happening? At that time, I was in the best shape of my adult life. I had stopped drinking for several months and everything was going well personally and professionally. After the doctor's diagnosis, it felt as if the ground beneath me had vanished.

I don't know how long I sat there, frozen. That minute seemed like an eternity. The doctor's voice gradually pulled me back to reality. "You'll need to be admitted within a few days to prepare for the surgery," he said in a patient tone, placing a hand on my shoulder. I managed a smile, got up, nodded, said thank you, and then talked to the nurses and administrative folks about scheduling. I was so shocked that I cannot even recall what they said to me.

When I finally left the hospital and got into my car to drive home, the gravity of the situation hit me like a shock wave. I pulled over and began to cry, overwhelmed with sadness and fear. The thought of a tumor—rogue cells clumping together inside my head and potentially killing me—was unbearable. I sat in my car for a long time, staring at the steering wheel, unable to move even after I had reached home and parked.

After a while, I got up and went inside. I picked up my phone; my mom was the first person I called. As soon as I heard her voice, the tears returned. I told her everything, and we cried together over the phone. "We'll get through this," she said. "You're strong, and you're not alone. My prayers are with you. I'm coming to you." I could hear her sobbing hysterically.

After hanging up, I called my dad. His confident response was, "You will get through this, Captain." It was a short but tough message that I really needed to hear at that moment. Next, I reached out to my closest friends, knowing I could count on them for support during this difficult period. My thoughts then turned to my brother Khatib, whose unwavering loyalty and understanding have always strengthened me. I also thought of my fraternity brothers and West Point classmates, who have stood by me through thick and thin, providing laughter when I needed it most and a sense of camaraderie that always lifts my spirits. Each of them has played a crucial role in my life, offering a unique mix of encouragement and practical advice.

As I reflected on all our shared experiences, I found comfort in knowing I wouldn't face this journey alone. Their collective strength and unwavering support gave me hope, and I felt grateful for the ways they each contributed to my life, especially as I grappled with the fears and uncertainties surrounding my diagnosis and upcoming brain surgery.

FINDING STRENGTH IN ADVERSITY

After feeling sad for several days, my sadness transformed into anger. I stared at the ceiling of my apartment, thinking, *Why me? Why now?* I had already endured so much. People depended on me to stay strong and continue my success; they relied on me for financial support, guidance, and to be someone they could count on to be "there," wherever "there" might be.

I was still grappling with PTSD, trying to reintegrate myself back into a normal life. In that moment, I felt a sharp pain in my chest. This pain was not just emotional; it was physical too. Tears streamed down my face as I whispered, "Why? Haven't I been through enough?"

As the days passed, something began to shift within me. A calmness seeped into my soul like a small light breaking through a dark cloud. My thoughts started to change. I reflected on the lessons I had learned growing up in the South—as a paperboy, on the football field, in the military, and during my time in Kosovo and Iraq. Every challenge and obstacle had shaped me into the person I was. This tumor, as terrifying as it was, felt like just another test of my will and faith.

I began to think about the road ahead. Yes, it was going to be difficult. The surgery and recovery would not be easy, but I wasn't ready to give up. This was merely another roadblock on my journey through life. If life had taught me anything, it was that roadblocks are not the end; they are just temporary stops meant to slow you down and make you stronger.

I made the decision then and there that I would face this head-on. I would have the surgery, recover, and get back to living my life. There were still so many things I wanted to do and many dreams I had yet to chase. This tumor was not going to stop me; I made that decision in an instant.

In that moment, I felt a strange sense of peace. It didn't erase my fear or sadness, but it gave me something to hold onto: hope. Deep down, I had always sensed that something was wrong with my health. For years, I had a nagging feeling that there was an issue. The headaches, the hoarseness, the moments when my body didn't feel quite like my own—those symptoms finally added up. But I kept brushing them aside, convincing myself I was overthinking things.

When the doctor diagnosed me with a brain tumor, it felt as though my gut feeling had been validated. The CT scan did not just provide a diagnosis; it offered clear and undeniable proof that I wasn't imagining things. If I had to face a tumor, this was the best time for me to do it. I had proudly served my country, was still young and fit, and if things went well, I had plenty of time to pursue other dreams armed with my West Point diploma and military experience.

Despite my fear, I felt a sense of relief. A tumor the size of a golf ball is certainly serious, and the thought of undergoing brain surgery was overwhelming. However, at least I finally had an answer.

Once the initial shock wore off, I realized I had two choices: I could either let this diagnosis break me, or I could fight back. I chose to fight. To do that, I needed strength—not just physical strength but also mental, spiritual, and emotional strength. I found that strength by trusting the process.

I reminded myself that I was not alone in this. My surgeons were world-renowned, skilled doctors who knew what they were doing, and my family and friends supported me. I decided to be optimistic and let the doctors do their job.

Within two weeks of receiving the life-changing news, I was being prepped for brain surgery at Walter Reed Medical Center. I was nervous, of course, but also strangely calm. I had decided to trust the process, and now it was time to put that trust to the test.

A SECOND CHANCE

The night before my surgery, my mother arrived late, and we cried together when she got there. The next day, as I was about to go into surgery, my friends and family wished me luck, tears welling in their eyes. Everyone understood that this surgery was life-threatening; brain surgery is always considered high-risk due to the intricate and delicate nature of the brain and nervous system. Any damage that occurs during the procedure can lead to serious complications, such as infection, bleeding, blood clots, seizures, stroke, or neurological deficits.

One of the saddest and scariest moments of my life was signing a document acknowledging these risks hours before my surgery. Here I was, a person who had built my legacy on fitness, signing a paper that stated that if I survived the surgery, I might not be able to engage in the physical activities that had improved my life and that of my family. This thought was extremely depressing.

After receiving warm wishes from friends and family, the doctor put me under anesthesia, and I fell into a deep sleep. The surgery was initially estimated to last at least twelve hours, but it ended up taking eighteen. Being under anesthesia felt like an out-of-body experience—it was as if I entered another world where time did not exist.

While my body lay still on the operating table, my mind transported me to an unexpected and beautiful place. I found myself sitting on the front porch of a familiar house in Adams Run, South Carolina. The sun was shining, and the air was filled with the smell of fresh-cut grass and the faint scent of cigars.

Sitting across from me in his old rocking chair, sipping whiskey and puffing on a cigar, was my favorite person—my beloved Granddaddy J.D. Seeing him felt incredibly real, as if no time had passed since we were last together. He had that same twinkle in his eye and mischievous grin. "Well, if it isn't Omar," he said, leaning back in his chair. "What are you doing here, boy?" I couldn't help but smile. "I don't even know, Granddaddy J.D.," I replied. "But it's good to see you, sir."

I asked him for some Pappy Van Winkle whiskey, and he agreed, pouring me a generous glass. My granddad and I spent hours together that day.

We went fishing and played chess, and I lightly teased him about not having his will in order and about leaving his store to my mom. I also playfully chided him for keeping cash in a mattress, explaining that when he passed, he left me with the immense task of trying to rebuild the generational wealth that was lost while also contending with the generational trauma he had never made a serious effort to confront.

He joked about the summers I spent working as a cashier in his store as a kid. "Almost free labor," he chuckled. "You were both the cheapest and best help I ever had. You never complained and always applied yourself. Although, you did eat more than your fair share of cookies and chips and drank all the orange soda." He added this with a wide grin.

But then, he suddenly grew quiet. He leaned forward, rested a hand on my shoulder, and looked me straight in the eyes. "Omar," he said softly, "you have to go back." I didn't want to leave.

"But why?" I asked.

"Because your work isn't done yet," he replied. "There are still people who need you. There are things you need to do. It is not your time, boy." I was frustrated; I was enjoying just hanging out with my favorite person, free of worries.

Before I could express anything else, everything around me started to fade. When I opened my eyes, I saw my brother and father standing over me, their faces creased with worry. I tried to speak, but no words came out. My throat was dry, and the pain in my head was overwhelming.

Their relief at seeing me awake was palpable. I was back. I was alive. An overwhelming sense of gratitude washed over me. I attempted to wiggle my toes and move my arms, but nothing worked at that moment. My dad and brother reassured me that I would be okay, and the nurse reminded me that recovery would take time and there were still many unknowns they needed to test. However, one thing was clear: I had been given a second chance, and I wouldn't waste it.

THE ROAD TO RECOVERY

When I came to after the surgery, I woke up to a new reality. My body felt broken in ways I could never have imagined. Half my face was paralyzed, leaving me unable to smile or blink appropriately on one side. I had to drink through a straw because I could not close my mouth enough to sip through a glass. I couldn't walk, and swallowing without food going down the "wrong pipe" and chocking me felt like an impossible task.

My back throbbed with pain from the lumbar puncture so severe that even slight movements in the hospital bed were difficult. The left side of my head had a large, raw wound from the surgery. I was completely deaf in my left ear, and the constant ringing on that side was unsettling. Additionally, my left vocal cord was paralyzed, which made swallowing a challenge. Every sip of water and every attempt at eating was difficult, and most of the time, I couldn't keep anything down.

The doctors didn't sugarcoat it. They informed me I would likely need months of recovery at the hospital and it would take a long time to regain essential functions—if I could regain them at all. While I nodded politely, I thought to myself that there was no way I would stay in this hospital for months. The hospital was noisy, with constant foot traffic, and every hour a nurse would come in to check on me or my roommate. I resolved to get out of the hospital in eight weeks or less.

Walter Reed Medical was where many of the most seriously injured soldiers from Iraq and Afghanistan were treated. It had a reputation for excellent care, but as I mentioned, it was an extremely busy place. Being so close to Washington, DC, it attracted a lot of attention, with senators, generals, and politicians regularly coming to shake hands with patients and express their gratitude for our service.

I remember lying in my hospital bed, throbbing in pain, when a small group of high-ranking officials and some politicians walked through the ward. They wore bright smiles and extended firm handshakes, but I could see the sadness in their eyes as they looked at the soldiers who had lost limbs or suffered devastating injuries.

As I lay there, I couldn't help but think about the other patients around me. Many of them had injuries far worse than mine. Some had lost arms or legs, while others were dealing with severe burns or injuries that left them barely recognizable. Each day in that hospital felt like reliving the horrors of war. I knew I needed to get out of there as quickly as possible to reclaim my life.

After a couple weeks at Walter Reed, I began to notice small changes. One of the first things I focused on was reducing my morphine intake. Initially, the pain was so intense I relied on it to get through the day, pressing the morphine button every five minutes, even though I suspected it was regulated. Even if it was, there was something comforting about being able to press that button.

However, I knew I didn't want to depend on it or any other pain medication indefinitely. Gradually, I started pressing the button less and learning to endure the pain. This was far from easy, especially in the beginning. Every movement still hurt, and some days it felt like my body was screaming at me. Yet, each time I resisted the urge to press the morphine button, it felt like a small victory. I also noticed that I became less groggy and started to feel more like my normal self.

My appetite was not great, but I knew I needed to eat to regain my strength. Before the surgery, I had weighed 195 pounds, but at this point, I had dropped to 165 pounds. To help myself, I focused on consuming as much Jell-O, mashed potatoes, and protein shakes as possible. These became my everyday meals. They were soft and easy to swallow, which was important because my left vocal cord was still paralyzed and would require another surgery a few months later. Each bite took effort, but I persisted in eating consistently. The food wasn't exciting, but it was essential fuel for my body, and I needed every bit of strength I could get.

Despite the physical pain, something inside me shifted. Mentally, I started to see a way forward. The first few days after surgery had been rough. I felt stuck, overwhelmed, and unsure of how to improve. But as the days turned into weeks, I realized that recovery was possible. It would not be fast, and it would not be easy, but it was possible.

THE HOSPITAL TEST, PASSED

The physical pain was still present, but mentally, I felt stronger. I began to think about all the people rooting for me: my family, my friends, and even the hospital staff. They believed in me, and I didn't want to disappoint them. Most importantly, I didn't want to disappoint myself.

I envisioned my future: walking again, smiling, and fully living my life. That vision became my motivation. My determination to move forward stemmed from my desire to accomplish more—not just for myself but for the people who counted on me.

One of my most significant sources of motivation was my mother. Over the years, she had faced many health challenges, and as her caretaker, I had taken on a role that extended beyond simply being her son. I managed her bills, appointments, and various daily tasks. She relied on me, and I took that responsibility seriously. Lying in that hospital bed, I often thought about her. I imagined her at home, worrying about me and wondering how she would manage everything without my help. That thought weighed heavily on me. I couldn't let her down at any cost. She needed me, and I needed to get better for her.

That's when I realized that my responsibilities were among the main reasons I needed to recover. They were my biggest motivators, providing me with a reason to push through the pain and take the complicated steps toward healing. As I focused on my recovery, I knew I needed a clear goal to work toward. Simply sitting in the hospital bed day after day wouldn't bring me back to life. So, I asked my doctor, "What must I do to get out of here?"

He paused thoughtfully before responding, "If you can use your walker to make it around the entire floor, that will show us you're strong enough to go home." It sounded simple, but I knew it wouldn't be easy. Standing for just a few minutes left me breathless and shaky. My back had an open wound from the lumbar puncture, and my head was filled with stitches. My legs felt weak, and my body was still recovering from surgery and medication. The thought of walking around the entire floor seemed impossible, but I told myself I had to try.

The next day, I made my first attempt. A nurse helped me out of bed and handed me the walker. Just standing there holding onto it felt like a workout. My arms trembled, and my legs felt like jelly. But I inhaled deeply and took my first step. After a few steps, my body protested. My back throbbed, legs burned, and head felt heavy. I had to stop and sit down after what felt like an eternity.

For the next three weeks, I tried again every day, pushing myself a little further each time. There were days I felt like I was making no progress, which was frustrating. My body hurt, and my energy levels were low. However, every setback taught me something, and every step brought me closer to my goal.

The nurses and staff became my cheerleaders, offering smiles and words of encouragement as I shuffled down the hall. "You got this, Captain Ritter," one of them said. "Just keep going." Their support made a huge difference.

Finally, about six weeks after my surgery, everything came together. With my walker, I started my trek around the floor. Step by step, I focused on my breathing, pacing myself, and staying steady. My legs shook, my back ached, and sweat poured down my face, but I didn't stop. My heart pounded with excitement as I reached the final stretch of the loop. When I crossed the finish line, I could hardly believe it—I had done it. I had walked around the entire floor.

The next day, the doctors came to my room with good news. "You're ready to go home," they said. Hearing those words felt like a victory. I had fought through so much pain and strife to reach this point, and now, I was finally going home.

CHAPTER 10 TRIGGERS

Reflecting on the events of this period, the diagnosis of my brain tumor was undoubtedly the most significant and life-altering trigger I've ever faced. It wasn't just the news itself—it was the cascade of emotions, realizations, and physical challenges that followed, each of which contributed to the mental-health struggles I would carry forward.

- The moment the doctor told me I had a brain tumor the size of a golf ball pressing against critical nerves, my world came to a standstill. I remember sitting in his office, frozen, unable to process the words. "You need surgery immediately," he said, and those words echoed in my mind like a thunderclap. I had always prided myself on my physical fitness and resilience, but this diagnosis shattered that image. It was a stark reminder that no matter how strong I thought I was, my body was vulnerable. That realization was terrifying and left me feeling powerless.
- Driving home after the diagnosis was another trigger. I pulled over and cried, overwhelmed by the thought of something growing inside my head, consuming my life. The fear of the unknown—what the surgery would entail, whether I would survive, and how my life would change—was suffocating. I felt like I was staring into an abyss, and the weight of it was almost too much to bear.
- Calling my mom and dad to share the news was another deeply emotional moment. Hearing my mom sob hysterically and my dad's confident yet brief reassurance brought out a mix of emotions: grief, fear, and a sense of responsibility. Their reactions reminded me how much they depended on me, and the thought of letting them down added to the pressure I was already feeling. I knew I had to be strong for them, but inside, I felt anything but strong.
- The days leading up to the surgery were filled with triggers that heightened my anxiety. Signing the document acknowledging the risks of brain surgery was one of the hardest moments for me. Reading the list of potential complications—such as infection, bleeding, seizures, stroke, or permanent neurological deficits—felt like staring at the worst-case scenarios for my life. The thought that I might lose the ability to engage in physical activities, which had been such a core part of my identity, was devastating. It felt like I was signing away the person I was.
- The surgery itself, lasting eighteen hours, was a surreal experience. While I was under anesthesia, I had a vivid dream of sitting on the porch with my Granddaddy J.D., fishing and playing chess. It felt so real, and when he told me, "You have to go back," I knew I couldn't

give up. That dream was both a comfort and a trigger—it reminded me of the life I still had to live and the people who needed me, but it also underscored the gravity of what I was facing.
- Waking up after the surgery was another trigger that shook me to my core. My body felt broken in ways I couldn't have imagined. Half my face was paralyzed, I couldn't walk, and I was completely deaf in my left ear. Drinking through a straw and struggling to swallow were humbling experiences that made me feel like a shadow of my former self. The physical pain was overwhelming, but the emotional toll of seeing myself in such a state was even harder to bear. I couldn't help but wonder if I would ever recover or regain the life I once had.
- The road to recovery was filled with triggers that tested my mental strength. The pain, the inability to move or eat properly, and the constant ringing in my deaf ear were daily reminders of how much I had lost. Even small victories, like cutting back on morphine or walking with a walker, were bittersweet. Each step forward was a reminder of how far I still had to go.

Through it all, the brain tumor diagnosis and its aftermath forced me to confront my vulnerability, fears, and identity. It wasn't just a physical battle—it was a mental and emotional one that reshaped how I saw myself and the world around me. This chapter of my life was a turning point, and while it was filled with pain and uncertainty, it also taught me the importance of resilience, self-advocacy, and finding strength in adversity.

CHAPTER 11

DETOUR AHEAD

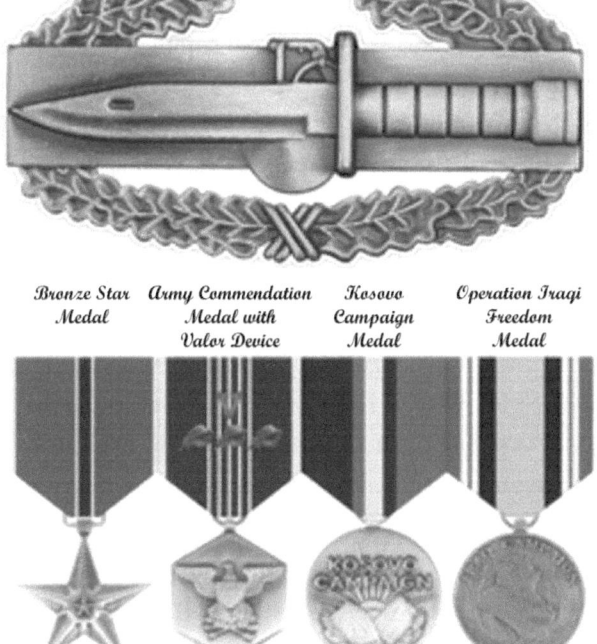

My most cherished military awards

Recovering from brain surgery was a significant challenge. There were days I felt incredibly fatigued or experienced severe headaches, making even simple tasks like getting out of bed difficult. A crucial part of my recovery involved rest, strict adherence to medical advice, and reliance on the support of my family and friends to heal properly. As the months passed, I began to regain my strength and adjust to my new normal. This adjustment wasn't easy, but my grit, patience, and perseverance made all the difference in helping me get through it.

After my release from the hospital, I had weekly follow-up appointments. These visits were significant milestones in my recovery, and I often looked forward to hearing about my progress. They were also opportunities to learn from medical professionals about the treatments and medications I needed to support my healing. I hoped that eventually, I would be able to return to my role as a military officer.

Unfortunately, reality hit me during one particular doctor's visit. I walked into the clinic feeling hopeful and excited, as I had finally reached a point where I could walk without support. Deep down, I wanted this visit to be the one where the doctor told me I was completely healthy and tumor-free and could return to my normal life within the next several months.

When the doctor entered the room, I was optimistic and ready for what I thought would be good news. However, what he told me turned my world upside down. The doctor explained that due to the surgery, I had sustained several injuries from which I would not recover. I would never regain hearing in my left ear, my left vocal cord was paralyzed, my headaches would not subside, and the significant atrophy of my trapezius muscle, along with some nerve damage, was permanent. To complicate matters, a piece of my skull had been removed to assess the tumor. He informed me that due to these injuries, I would need to be medically retired from the military. I realized that my military career was over.

I had joined the military to be a combat arms officer and lead soldiers into combat. The thrill, purpose, and camaraderie had drawn me to this path; it was not just a career to me but also my passion and my identity. When the doctor told me this path was no longer a viable one, it felt like losing a part of myself. Even if I had not planned to stay on active duty for twenty years or more, I had imagined myself in the Army Reserves or National Guard, serving my country in some capacity. I sat there stunned and anxious, processing everything. My body had gone through a lot during the surgery, and now, it felt as though my mind and spirit were being tested as well.

I thought to myself, *What will I do now? How can I adjust to this new reality?* I left the clinic that day knowing my life would never be the same.

I returned home feeling completely distressed. My mind raced, and my heart felt heavy. The idea of losing my identity as an army officer did not sit well with me. I had joined the military with a vision of leading soldiers, actively serving, and making a difference. I felt ill-prepared to transition to a life outside the military so soon. I thought I had a choice in the matter, but the option of staying in the military had been taken away from me.

As I sat in my apartment, I felt lost and overwhelmed. Thoughts of my future swirled in my head. How could I adjust to a life I was not prepared for? How would I find the same sense of purpose and pride?

Despite enduring the challenges of combat and the immense ordeal of brain surgery, I found it disheartening that no one had recommended or mandated mental-health counseling for me. It felt as if I was merely going through the motions, expected to adjust seamlessly to each new reality. The repercussions of such drastic changes were significant, yet there was a stark silence around the importance of mental-health support. As I grappled with the emotional weight of my diagnosis and the sudden shift in my identity, I couldn't shake the feeling that taking care of my mental well-being was just as crucial as the physical healing I was undergoing. It left me questioning how many others were in my position, navigating their struggles alone without the guidance or support they desperately needed.

In my despair, a memory resurfaced that night. I recalled a conversation with my fraternity brother and West Point classmate Andrew Glaze. Right after we graduated from West Point, he told me about his plan to take the Graduate Management Admissions Test (GMAT), which is required for business school. He had decided to follow in the footsteps of his older brother, who had graduated from Princeton University and become a successful business executive.

I had grown up believing I would spend twenty or more years in the military, whether full-time or reserve, aspiring to be a high-ranking military officer. However, that conversation stuck with me, and I decided that perhaps business was an option I could pursue after my medical retirement. As a result, I began networking to gain a deeper understanding of the business world and determine the best way to make the transition.

OPENING THE NEXT DOOR

It is often said that when one door closes, another opens, and I had to come to terms with the idea of going in a different direction. My focus shifted to attending business school to reinvent myself and discover a new purpose in life. From the days at Granddaddy J.D.'s store, I had been drawn to the concept of business, influenced by my grandfather's entrepreneurial spirit.

Additionally, my favorite courses at West Point—where I had managed to earn the elusive A—had been Principles of Finance, Management Practice, and Human Resource Management. These classes felt natural, as they involved understanding human motivations and measuring results. They also reminded me of my time as a paperboy, successfully turning a small opportunity into significant income to help support my family. Reflecting on this gave me hope. Perhaps this was the path I was meant to take all along. A faint smile spread across my face as the wheels started turning in my head; I was determined to turn this negative experience into a positive outcome.

At this point, I threw all my energy into studying for the GMAT. Diving into studying took my mind off everything else, as I had limited time between taking the test and applying to business school. I set my sights on attending an Ivy League business school, and I needed an excellent GMAT score.

The maximum GMAT score was 800, and the average scores at Ivy League schools were 700 or higher. This meant I needed to score exceptionally well on the test to have a chance at admission. Initially, I thought I could study for just a week or so and achieve a good score. I tried this and ended up with a score of 550. The GMAT gave me a dose of humility.

Realizing my initial approach wasn't working, I reassessed my strategy and decided to cut myself off from the outside world to focus on studying. I took a recovery leave of absence and locked myself in my house for an entire month. I gathered every practice test I could find and resolved not to retake the GMAT until I could consistently score at least 750 on the practice tests.

After a month of dedicated studying and solid scores on my practice tests, I finally decided it was time to try again. I scheduled my test at a random test center in Nyack, New York. With the GMAT, you receive your score immediately at the testing site. On test day, I poured all my energy into the exam, ensuring I read each question carefully and felt confident about my answers. When I finished the test, I was nervous but hopeful that I had achieved a higher score.

When I received my score this time, both the test center proctor and I were shocked and excited about the results. My score had improved significantly, giving me a real shot at an Ivy League business school.

THE FELDBERG FELLOWSHIP

Posing with Meyer Feldberg, dean emeritus, Columbia Business School

I immediately began applying to business schools and decided that Columbia Business School would be the best fit for me. The school had a strong admissions committee, I enjoyed spending time with the current students, and its New York location allowed me to continue seeing my doctor at West Point and take advantage of the excellent facilities at the New York Veterans Administration (VA) Hospital. New York City, being the business capital of the world, allowed me to immerse myself in the business world and maximize my chances of seamlessly entering corporate America.

I started school just a few months after my brain surgery, which, in hindsight, was far too soon. Initially, I had planned to postpone my enrollment for a year; however, Columbia Business School awarded me the prestigious Feldberg Fellowship.

The Feldberg Fellowship is one of Columbia Business School's most esteemed grants, awarded each year to select entering students who demonstrate outstanding leadership potential and a history of academic excellence, particularly those with backgrounds in entrepreneurship, finance, military service, and social enterprise. The fellowship and its accompanying financial support were nontransferable to the following year, which meant I had to make a critical decision regarding my finances as well as my health. Consequently, I decided to persevere and enter business school, even though my mind and body were not fully ready.

At the start of school, I had recovered about 60 percent, and every passing day reminded me of the ongoing recovery process. I was still healing and managing excruciating pain with multiple opioids, such as Percocet and antiemetics, while also being cautious to not become dependent on these drugs.

During business school, there were many nights I experienced such intense pain I couldn't sleep or study. At times, I was too affected by the opioids I was taking to participate in focus groups or classes. Despite these challenges, I never mentioned my struggles and did my best to push through the first semester.

Looking back, I realize that if I had known then what I know now, I would have postponed my attendance. The financial benefits of starting a year early would have been easily outweighed by the advantages of entering business school fully healthy. It would have also been beneficial to address my mental and physical health before tackling such a demanding academic environment.

That said, I must acknowledge how much I owe to Columbia Business School. The fellowship alleviated some of the financial stress of attending such a prestigious institution. The admissions committee recognized my leadership experience and what I overcame in the military, and I am grateful that they thoroughly reviewed every application and selected mine from thousands based on my unique experiences.

The challenges I had faced, which contributed to my significant mental-health issues, also inspired me to write a passionate admissions essay about my life story. This ultimately led to my acceptance to this esteemed institution. I truly value being a member of the Feldberg Fellows group, a unique community of individuals striving to make meaningful change in the world. The fellowship has allowed me to engage in conversations with Dean Meyer Feldberg and connect with visionaries like Michael Kopko, who is making a difference in patient support through his company, Pearl Health.

COLUMBIA BUSINESS SCHOOL BRILLIANCE

I was excited to be part of Columbia Business School's Class of 2007. However, after a couple weeks of classes, it became clear I was academically far behind the average student in terms of business acumen. I realized I would need to work exceptionally hard to learn the material and graduate.

Here are the facts: People who attend Ivy League business schools are incredibly driven. One classmate might aim to take over their family's global business, while another aspires to become a school superintendent or the executive director of a nonprofit organization. Others may have ambitions to become lawyers, medical doctors, entertainers, etc., all with the help of the prestige that comes with earning an MBA from Columbia Business School. You cannot predict where anyone will end up over time.

I would estimate about 95 percent of the students entering elite business schools have a clear idea of what they want to do with their degree in the short term and, to some extent, even in the medium term. For these individuals, business school is primarily about networking, focusing on a few key courses, and opening doors or, at the very least, improving their credentials.

Columbia's role for these students is to connect them with recruiters, classmates, and leaders from their target industries. Not to mention, some of my classmates had already led companies, bought and sold businesses, or sat on public boards. For instance, if someone had spent time working as an investment banker, they were not attending business school to refine their skills. They were already well versed in market trends, capital strategies, and the intricacies of the financial world. For them, the coursework was merely a review of what they had been doing for years. They were experts, laser-focused on their goals, which typically centered around careers in private equity or venture capital or strategic roles that change businesses.

Then there was me. I hadn't engaged in any academic work for years. I could assemble a weapon with my eyes closed, navigate using a map and an eight-digit grid, and lead a unit in combat. Yet here I was, among these brilliant individuals, dealing with my own challenges, including headaches from a brain surgery incision and PTSD, which I had yet to treat.

Most of my classmates graduated from college and immediately focused on creating financial reports and corporate strategies. They read *The Wall Street Journal* and understood the complexities of global business. Meanwhile, my expertise was in directing movement on the battlefield to outmaneuver the enemy. While this was a valuable skill, it didn't help me understand accounting or contribute to a company's profits.

When I first arrived at business school, I didn't even know what a corporate tax rate was. I had no understanding of the fundamentals of finance or business. I couldn't tell you what a C-suite was or who occupied it. I hadn't heard of Goldman Sachs, Lehman Brothers, the Carlyle Group, or even Warren Buffett and Jamie Dimon. Meanwhile, most of my classmates admired these global brands and their leaders.

The first six months were overwhelming. I felt like I was constantly playing catch-up, just trying to keep my head above water. It reminded me of being a plebe at West Point, struggling to keep up academically. To make matters worse, the first semester was a crucial period for internship recruiting. By the end of the first semester, first-year students were expected to have made connections to secure summer internships that would shape our futures after business school.

However, instead of focusing entirely on recruiting, I desperately needed to concentrate on my classwork while also recovering and dealing with constant headaches and pain from my surgery. My ability to network with my classmates was significantly impacted.

Every Thursday, there was a happy hour for the business school. However, I could rarely attend because I was either studying or recovering. Furthermore, these happy hours involved a good amount of drinking, and I couldn't eat or drink in public without feeling sick. I would throw up if I tried to eat and drink while networking. Additionally, I didn't want to go back to overconsuming alcohol, especially since I was no longer in peak condition.

Let me be clear: It is really challenging to network with tipsy people when you are sober. I did my best to build meaningful relationships, but I must admit that I earned a C in the "getting to know your classmates" part of business school. As a result, I felt like I was swimming against the current in my recruiting efforts.

LIFE IS A MARATHON

The good news is that life is not a sprint; it's a marathon. I frequently reminded myself of this to stay motivated during my time at Columbia, where I found myself surrounded by some of the most competitive individuals on the planet. I committed to learning from them while also sharing my own leadership experience.

Despite having already faced significant challenges—fighting in a war and undergoing brain surgery—I still felt intimidated during those first few months at business school. In conversations, I often struggled to find my voice as my classmates discussed the latest market shifts, the future of tech companies, and evolving consumer behavior. It felt like they were speaking a foreign language, and I found myself lost in translation.

I refused to let myself feel too down. Instead, I focused on the skills I did possess, such as leadership, resilience, and critical thinking. While I may not have been a finance expert or a corporate executive, I excelled at making tough decisions and handling pressure.

I took comfort in the thought that many of my classmates likely couldn't manage the intense combat training and war fighting that had brought me to this point. This realization motivated me to bridge the gap in my business knowledge. While the concepts were complex and the workload relentless, I was determined not to let the steep learning curve defeat me.

Reflecting on my experiences, I acknowledged that the challenges of business school, while substantial, did not compare to the intensity of my first semester at West Point. That experience had felt like jumping into the deep end, facing both academic and physical obstacles.

When business school presented hurdles, I leaned on the discipline I had developed in the military. I understood I didn't need to learn everything at once; my priority was to identify and focus on what mattered most. This approach enabled me to enhance my skills in prioritizing, breaking tasks into manageable parts, and cultivating patience with myself.

I also took advantage of the strong sense of community within Ivy League institutions. Many Wall Street experts generously took time out of their busy schedules to help those of us without a business background. I am incredibly grateful to my classmates for dedicating their time to explaining concepts, answering questions, and guiding us through challenging principles. Their support made a significant difference in our academic journeys.

JOHN HAMPTON'S SHARED WISDOM

The corporate recruiting landscape in business school can be incredibly challenging, yet it's a topic seldom discussed. Many of my classmates excelled at networking; they could enter an event, connect with key individuals within just twenty minutes, and leave knowing their interactions would leave a lasting impression on the companies present. For the rest of us, however, the pressure to effectively network and engage the right people to secure coveted internships was immense. When I approached executives at these networking sessions, it often felt like they were speaking a different language, addressing concepts I was expected to master in my second year, not just three months into my first.

Through my experiences, I quickly learned that companies—whether they are banks, consulting firms, or Fortune 500 corporations—carefully monitor every interaction during the recruiting process. They tend to extend internship offers to the most intelligent and talented candidates first. If those offers are declined, they then consider the next group of candidates. Compounding this situation is the fact that if a company faces a choice between two individuals with similar academic qualifications, they almost always select the one who has attended the most events, engaged in face-to-face interactions, and demonstrated a genuine commitment to forming connections. Why does this matter? It reflects dedication to the organization and suggests a higher likelihood of accepting a job if offered. Acceptance rates are crucial for these companies, so they meticulously track figures to evaluate the return on investment from their recruitment efforts.

I vividly remember the moment I recognized the importance of networking. I had a project due, and a networking event at a major bank's headquarters coincided with a particularly busy week. I found myself torn between staying to complete the project and attending the event.

It was then that my mentor John Hampton—an executive at Citibank who graduated from West Point and Columbia Business School years before me—called to impart an invaluable lesson. He reminded me that I was no longer in the army and that succeeding in the business world required more than just hard work. To enter a top company, making difficult choices was essential, and attending recruiting events was a critical factor in landing a job after business school. John explained the importance of building relationships and encouraged me to take on this challenge.

He recounted his own internship recruitment experience, emphasizing the necessity of being present at every event and networking with as many individuals as possible. "When it came time to make offers," he shared, "they remembered me. I stood out because I was consistently present, asking questions and actively engaging with the recruiters. That commitment makes a huge difference."

The conversation I had with John marked a turning point in my life. I came to the realization that excelling academically would not be enough on its own. Columbia was not like West Point; everyone was knowledgeable, and achieving honors seemed out of my reach. Although accepting this fact was challenging, I eventually came to terms with it. I quickly redirected my focus, dedicating a significant amount of time to networking in hopes of securing a valuable internship.

THE BUSINESS SCHOOL THAT NEVER SLEEPS

One of my most vivid memories of Columbia Business School is of the constant energy and excitement that pulsed through every corner of the campus. There was an unmistakable buzz, whether I was in the classroom, studying in the library, or grabbing lunch in the cafeteria. It wasn't just the typical hustle of students completing assignments; it was an energy focused on the question, "What's next to accomplish?" People were always thinking about their next challenge, their next step, and the big ideas they wanted to pursue.

When I arrived at Columbia, I had no clear sense of my future. However, I quickly realized I had a bright path ahead and needed to consider what came next. The atmosphere at Columbia was contagious—it was impossible not to get swept up in it, even on days when I felt utterly exhausted.

Every conversation I had seemed to return to ambitious goals and plans. I saw people with fire in their eyes. Everywhere I looked, there were individuals driven to make a difference, always seeking new opportunities to learn and grow. It was a place where ambition was not just encouraged; it became part of the very air we breathed. I constantly reminded myself that I had earned my spot. Despite the challenges I faced, I was there for a reason.

The best part of my journey was the supportive classmates I met along the way. One day, my classmate Dan Heller, a top student, turned to me and said, "You know, it's awe-inspiring how you've jumped into this whole business thing, especially given your background. I'm sure it's a massive shift, but I have no doubt you will figure it out." His comment caught me off guard, but in a good way. "Thanks," I replied, smiling. "Yes, it's been a big transition, but I'm committed. I know there's a huge gap between being a soldier and a civilian in business. I'm glad I have Columbia to help me bridge that gap."

Learning finance and accounting at Columbia Business School was one of the most challenging yet rewarding experiences of my life. Columbia requires all students to take these core courses because finance is the "language" of business. That said, I had no idea they would be so time-consuming and difficult. The concepts were complex, and I often felt completely overwhelmed. The sheer volume of new information was staggering, and there were times when I truly felt like I was drowning in numbers, equations, and terms that made no sense at all.

There were moments when I seriously questioned whether I had made the right decision. Some nights, I would sit at my desk, staring blankly at my textbook, wondering if I would ever understand the material and hoping to learn through osmosis. The finance and accounting terms seemed to blur together, and I often thought, *What did I get myself into?*

It would have been easy to give up and say, "This isn't for me." I would have loved to pack everything up, hit reset, and take a break until I felt more prepared. However, despite all the challenges, I persevered. Something inside me would not let me quit. I aimed to learn enough to pass the courses and keep up with my classmates.

Every day, I faced challenges head-on, reread chapters, and sought help from my professors and classmates. I did everything I could to succeed. I even became weight-lifting partners with one of my professors, Dr. Levav, hoping his brilliance would inspire me. I attended extra office hours while others were out at the bar or relaxing. When things felt especially difficult, I reminded myself why I was there. This journey, with all its challenges, was meant to help me transition from being a soldier to becoming a civilian, and I was determined to make it work.

As I mentioned before, I probably should have given myself more time to adjust to civilian life and address my internal issues before taking on the pressures of a rigorous academic program and intensive job recruiting. However, having just survived several life-or-death situations, I was determined not to put my dreams on hold any longer than necessary. My awareness of my mortality made me realize how short life is, so I decided to go for it. Although it was tough, I'm proud of myself for pushing through. It required a lot of grit. There were many nights I felt overwhelmed and doubted my ability to succeed, but I kept moving forward. Even when I felt utterly out of my depth, I reminded myself that I had made it this far and could overcome this challenge too.

IGNORING THE DOCTOR'S ORDERS

I felt an intense sense of pride when the first semester of business school came to an end and I had successfully passed all my courses. I had faced challenges that often felt insurmountable but emerged victorious. Additionally, I had secured an internship in the investment banking division at Bank of America for the upcoming summer.

I was fortunate to have a mentor, Joe Beard, who was an alumnus of both West Point and Columbia Business School. Despite his demanding schedule of working sixteen hours a day and caring for his three-year-old, Joe woke me up at 5:30 a.m. to prepare me for my interviews. Sometimes tough love is necessary, and Joe certainly provided that before the sun came up. Because of his guidance and despite my academic and health struggles, I landed a sought-after internship. I am forever grateful to him for his mentorship and guidance.

Regarding my health challenges, each time I would visit the doctor's office, he would sit me down and ask with genuine concern, "How are you handling the pressure of Columbia?" His eyes would soften as he studied my responses, trying to gauge my body language. He frequently cautioned me, saying, "Are you pushing yourself too hard? You've been through a lot. Your body needs time to heal, and you're putting a lot of pressure on it. Don't you think it might be time to slow down?"

I would look at him, feeling a knot tighten in my stomach, and then I would smile, attempting to convey that I had everything under control. The truth was far from that. The pressure to keep up with my classmates—the constant juggling of assignments, networking events, and exams—while my body was still recovering from the trauma of brain surgery was overwhelming. It was a bitter pill to swallow.

I still had not faced my demons from PTSD either. Despite this, I would respond with a fake chuckle, "You know, doc, you're right, but I can't help it. I've never been one to sit back. I've always pushed myself, even when it feels impossible. I don't think I can stop now."

The doctor would sigh and shake his head, looking almost sad. "I understand your drive, but your health must come first. You must listen to your body and give it the time it needs." I would nod and smile, but deep down, I knew I wouldn't take his advice. I wasn't the kind of person who could sit back and wait. Even if it meant fighting through the pain and pushing my limits, I was determined not to give up. Columbia was my chance to reinvent myself and prove I could succeed in corporate America.

There were days my head would throb painfully as I left the doctor's office. I often pondered whether I should slow down and take a step back. Yet, just as quickly, I would dismiss the thought. I couldn't stop now, especially after working so hard to get here and coming so far.

The day I graduated from Columbia Business School, I could not contain my joy. It was a moment of pure, unfiltered happiness—one that I had worked tirelessly for yet never truly believed would arrive. All the late nights, struggles, self-doubt, and relentless pressure had led to this moment, and it felt as if I had been reborn.

CHAPTER 11 TRIGGERS

Reflecting on this time in my life, I can clearly identify several triggers that arose, each of which deeply impacted my mental health and contributed to the challenges I would face later. These moments weren't just isolated events—they were pivotal experiences that shaped my emotional and psychological state.

- The first major trigger was when I learned the full extent of my injuries and the reality of my medical retirement from the military. Walking into that clinic, I was hopeful and excited, believing I was on the verge of returning to my normal life. Instead, the doctor's words shattered my world. Hearing that I would never regain hearing in my left ear, my vocal cord was paralyzed, and I had permanent nerve damage was devastating. But the hardest blow was being told I could no longer serve in the military.

- The military wasn't just a career for me—it was my identity, my purpose, and my passion. Losing that felt like losing a part of myself, and I left the clinic feeling stunned, anxious, and completely lost. That moment marked the beginning of a deep sense of grief and despair that I struggled to process.
- Another trigger was the overwhelming sense of uncertainty about my future. Sitting in my apartment after the doctor's visit, I felt completely distressed. My mind raced with questions: *What will I do now? How can I adjust to this new reality?* The idea of losing my identity as an army officer and transitioning to a civilian life I wasn't prepared for filled me with anxiety. I had always envisioned myself serving in some capacity, whether in active duty or the reserves, and now that option was gone. The weight of this realization was suffocating, and I felt ill-equipped to find a new sense of purpose and pride.
- The memory of my fraternity brother Andrew Glaze and his plan to pursue business school was both a trigger and a lifeline. On one hand, it reminded me of a path I had never considered before, but on the other, it forced me to confront the fact that my original dreams were no longer viable.
- While networking and exploring the business world gave me hope, it also highlighted the stark contrast between the life I had planned and the one I was now forced to live. This shift in focus was emotionally taxing as I grappled with the loss of my old identity while trying to build a new one.
- The decision to attend Columbia Business School so soon after my brain surgery was another significant trigger. While the Feldberg Fellowship was an incredible honor, the timing was far from ideal. I was

still recovering physically and mentally, managing excruciating pain with opioids and dealing with the risk of addiction.
- The demands of business school—studying, networking, and participating in study groups—were overwhelming, especially on nights when the pain was so severe I couldn't sleep or concentrate. I often felt like I was drowning, unable to keep up with my classmates or fully engage in the academic environment. In hindsight, I realize that pushing myself to attend school before I was ready only exacerbated my struggles, but at the time, I felt compelled to prove I could succeed despite the odds.
- The constant comparison to my classmates became a significant burden for me. Many of them were already experts in finance and business, while I was starting from scratch. I didn't even understand basic concepts like corporate tax rates nor did I know prominent figures such as Warren Buffett and Jamie Dimon. The steep learning curve made me feel inadequate and intimidated, leading me to question whether I truly belonged at Columbia. The pressure to catch up academically, combined with my physical recovery, created a relentless cycle of self-doubt and stress.
- Networking events, particularly the Thursday happy hours, became another source of anxiety. I couldn't drink or eat in public without throwing up, which made it difficult to connect with classmates and recruiters. My inability to participate fully in these social settings left me feeling isolated and out of place. I knew networking was crucial for securing internships and building relationships, but my health challenges made it nearly impossible to engage effectively. This disconnect added to my feelings of inadequacy and frustration.
- The physical symptoms I experienced—headaches, pain, and the lingering effects of brain surgery—were constant reminders of my limitations. Ignoring my doctor's advice to slow down and prioritize my health was a decision I made out of sheer stubbornness, but it came at a cost. The pressure to keep up with my classmates and prove myself in the business world often felt like a battle against my own body, and the toll it took on my mental health was significant.

Each of these triggers—the loss of my military career, the uncertainty about my future, the decision to attend business school prematurely, the constant comparisons to my classmates, the challenges of networking, and the physical symptoms—created a perfect storm of emotional and psychological strain. These moments weren't just challenges; they were deeply impactful experiences that shaped my mental health and forced me to confront the lasting effects of my injuries and loss of my identity.

CHAPTER 12

THE PATH FROM HERE

I WON'T RECOUNT EVERY COMPANY I HAVE EVER WORKED FOR nor delve into my entire employment history. However, I have been fortunate enough to reach the director level and above at industry giants like JPMorgan Chase, Wells Fargo, and TIAA. These experiences, among others, have provided me with valuable insights, but I would like to highlight some key points from my journey.

The average person who works at least forty hours a week spends about 20 percent of their life at work. Additionally, individuals typically spend around 33 percent of their lives sleeping. This leaves us with only 47 percent of our time to spend with friends and loved ones and engage in activities we enjoy.

Research indicates that the workplace can lead to various mental-health challenges, including work-related stress. Feelings of depression can arise from job dissatisfaction, a lack of work–life balance, isolation, and social alienation. Furthermore, bullying, harassment, and imposter syndrome can exacerbate these mental-health issues. Therefore, employers play a crucial role in creating supportive work environments and providing mental-health resources; however, it ultimately falls to employees to access these resources.

Reflecting on the importance of mental-health support in the workplace, I can personally attest to the challenges I faced at the start of my career after graduating from business school in May 2007. Although I was in better physical condition after recovering from brain surgery, I did not seek help for my PTSD, anxiety, and other mental-health issues during the two years I spent in business school. I failed to heed my doctor's advice, which, in hindsight, would have spared me a lot of pain and significantly reduced the time I suffered in silence. I am fortunate to be alive today to share my experiences with you.

THE INVESTMENT BANKING GRIND

I started my job at Bank of America in New York City after graduating from business school. I took pride in commuting on the subway from 118th Street and Frederick Douglass Boulevard to 9 West 57th Street. I enjoyed wearing the latest matching shirts and ties from Charles Tyrwhitt to work, even though I found myself sweating in the summer heat of the city. Most days, I operated on only four to five hours of sleep, whether it was from working late or enjoying the nightlife that my investment-banking colleagues and I often indulged in.

Two months into the role, I received what I initially thought was bad news: The bank needed me to move to Charlotte, North Carolina, to fill an investment banking associate opening on the southern team. They assured me my pay would remain the same, so I agreed to the move, as it would allow me to visit family in South Carolina when I had the time.

A typical workday for a young investment banker specializing in mergers and acquisitions began at 9:30 a.m. and often extended until 10:00 p.m. or later. When we were trying to secure a deal, my workday could stretch into the early hours of the following day. On average, I worked around ninety hours a week, including weekends. I even memorized the security code to my managing director's house because I was responsible for delivering presentation materials to his home if he had an early flight and we hadn't finished preparing the materials before he left at 6:00 p.m.

On one hand, the job paid extremely well, allowing me to finish paying off my mother's house within a year. On the other hand, I desperately needed sleep. There were times our team worked for two or three consecutive days. I remember working around the clock for a week straight as we tried to manage a multibillion-dollar metals and mining megamerger.

In the New York City office, this kind of relentless work was typical; there were always people in the office or out on the streets 24/7. However, Charlotte transformed into a ghost town at 6:00 p.m. on weekdays, with no sign of life on weekends. I also missed my associate group, as we spent so much time together that they doubled as my close friends with whom I would unwind.

In the demanding realm of mergers-and-acquisitions investment banking, where precision is paramount and the stakes are sky high, the additional challenges of isolation and extra stress in Charlotte complicated my role. Being physically separated from the fast-paced hub of the New York team heightened the pressure and magnified the need for meticulous attention to detail.

The high-octane environment of investment banking, where managing directors essentially function as persuasive salespeople, leaves no room for error. Every client presentation must be flawless, as even a minor mistake could spell disaster for a deal. In this fiercely competitive field, where senior bankers must outshine numerous rivals vying for the same business, the margin for error is indeed zero.

As a result, I found myself investing considerable time and effort into meticulously reviewing and refining presentations, triple-checking calculations, and ensuring that every detail was impeccable. My obsessive-compulsive disorder, often viewed as a hindrance elsewhere, emerged as a secret weapon in this challenging arena, guaranteeing error-free work when it mattered most.

Adding to this pressure, senior associates and vice presidents frequently assigned side projects to the junior team. These side projects were the things the senior bankers had no interest in—simply put, there was not enough money or benefit involved for them to care. Therefore, middle-level bankers would take them on in the hope of generating revenue to demonstrate to their bosses that they had the ability to grow the business.

By 2009, I was feeling immense mental-health pressure from the investment-banking grind. I struggled to maintain romantic relationships, was easily triggered, and often woke up in fear during the few hours of sleep I could manage. I distinctly remember one night waking up in a cold sweat, clutching my then-girlfriend as anxiety gripped me. Nevertheless, like many others, I kept working and did not seek help—even though the VA hospital was free for me and Bank of America offered excellent healthcare coverage. I was heading toward burnout; I recognized the signs but did nothing to save myself and improve my situation.

CULTURE SHOCK

In 2009, the global recession was transforming Wall Street. Several banks collapsed, and Bank of America acquired Merrill Lynch, renowned for its successful investment-banking division.

My managing director was reassigned to Canada, and after being laid off, I accepted a position on the active mergers-and-acquisitions team of a private company. In this role, I became heavily involved in creating various Excel models for the business, dedicating seven days a week to this task. I worked on all three financial statements, demonstrating a significant commitment to my work.

I collaborated closely with engineers and even developed a model to assess the return on investment for converting corn into ethanol. This role was essentially an extension of my previous experience in investment banking. By any standard, I was extremely successful in this position, excelling during my first year.

Although this company was one of the best run in the United States, I had to relocate for the position. My role at the bank had been eliminated, and there were no other "Wall Street"-type jobs available in 2009. I had my own mortgage to pay at that point, so I did what needed to be done. I accepted the job and put my home in Charlotte up for rent, as it had lost 40 percent of its value at the time.

The new company was the most homogeneous workplace I had ever experienced, not just in terms of ethnicity but also in culture. Having attended West Point and Columbia, I knew how to interact with different ethnicities and cultures, and being a minority never really impacted anything I had attempted to do in my adult life. However, there was a noticeable culture gap between me and most of my colleagues. Many of them were born and raised in Kansas, attended college in Kansas, and loved everything about life in Kansas. I did not mind that they loved the state of Kansas; heck, I love the United States. However, they expected everyone to assimilate to their culture; at least that is how I felt. I applauded their commitment to the company. In a way, it was similar to a soldier's commitment to the military. They were everything an employer would want in an employee: loyal, happy, and hard working. Further, the culture at this organization was strong, and all the employees had close-knit relationships with their coworkers and their coworkers' families. From the onset, it was clear I was an outsider or a hired hand who had come in to do one specific task: build merger-and-acquisition models.

Speaking of the culture, two weeks into my role, a colleague was getting off the elevator as I was getting on. I complimented her on her dress, and an hour later I was called into a meeting with a human resources leader for a brief on the workplace dos and don'ts. One of the don'ts: do not compliment individuals on their attire. This was all new to me, but I adjusted.

At the time, I was thirty-three years old and single. One day, as I strolled into the office and headed for my workspace, a coworker asked if I was married and had children. I replied "no" to both. She then asked if I was gay, and I quickly bolted to my office.

BAWSTIN

I could always count on friends and family, fraternity brothers, and acquaintances to visit me when I lived in New York and Charlotte. These visits gave me something to look forward to and helped take my mind off the everyday grind. However, no one was willing to come to this small Midwestern town to hang out with me. I typically worked Saturday mornings, which made it difficult to travel. The timing for flights was challenging, as every journey required a connection, and my department was always under tight deadlines. I felt stuck and trapped by the golden handcuffs of my salary.

After a year, the stress reached its peak. I experienced extreme anxiety about work, and my PTSD kept me awake at night; the migraines also returned. I hit rock bottom one evening while sitting on my bed with a 9mm pistol. I can't explain how I got to that point, but there I was. At that very moment, my good friend T. J. Pope called to check in on me. He likely has no idea that he saved my life that day.

Immediately after hanging up with T. J., I called the Veterans Crisis Line and spoke with an extremely helpful counselor. I sought the help I desperately needed. I began attending therapy sessions weekly, which helped me regain a positive mindset. Through counseling, I realized I needed to leave Wichita, Kansas. To clarify, my issue was never with the city itself; rather, it was that that place was not right for me at that point in my life given my state of mind. If I had pursued the proper treatment sooner, I would probably still be there because the company I worked for is the best in the industry. Mental-health issues often lead to many squandered opportunities both personally and professionally.

I made the decision to leave Wichita and began interviewing vigorously, eventually landing a job in Boston. The city was a breath of fresh air and helped me feel less isolated. I worked hard to create a vibrant social scene for myself in Boston while also giving back to the community. I was very active in the graduate chapter of Alpha Phi Alpha, participated in community service, and even conducted speaking sessions at local colleges to help students navigate their careers.

I met interesting people outside my immediate circle and connected with friends throughout the Northeast. I was back in the mix! However, I encountered a setback—I stopped going to counseling and fell back into old habits.

TOO MANY GONE TOO SOON

Cherish your people: My West Point classmates and brother at Army–LSU game in 2023

From 2010 to 2024, my journey was marked by significant professional growth and notable achievements, all while navigating a complex and evolving personal landscape. My career flourished as I earned continuous promotions within various organizations, attracting the attention of corporate recruiters eager to fill senior management roles at Fortune 100 companies.

I eventually rose to the prestigious position of senior finance and technology operations leader at J.P. Morgan Chase. Later, I served as the chief financial officer (CFO) for a business unit of a services company that successfully generated $1 billion in annual revenue.

Driven by a relentless pursuit of excellence, I placed a strong emphasis on enhancing my educational qualifications and professional credentials. I earned my Certified Public Accounting (CPA) license, obtained the Chartered Global Management Accountant (CGMA) designation, and became a Certified Exit Planning Advisor (CEPA). Additionally, I secured my Senior Professional in Human Resources (SPHR) certification, marking a significant milestone in my career. Building on this momentum, I committed to pursuing a doctorate in business administration (DBA), which I aim to complete by the end of 2026.

As I transitioned into my forties, my personal growth began to mirror my professional success. The pandemic shifted the dynamics of my life, allowing my girlfriend, Amanda, who is now my wife, to move with me into one of my homes in Summerville. In 2021, we took a significant step together by purchasing a house in Charlotte, and in 2022, we celebrated the arrival of our beloved child, Aviva. I also discovered a passion for golf in 2011, and it has become a cherished outlet for relaxation and mental clarity amid life's challenges.

Since 2023, I have dedicated myself to community service by serving on the Board of the Down Syndrome Association of Greater Charlotte and the Advisory Board of Teach for America (Charlotte–Piedmont–Triad). I also raise awareness among veterans, encouraging them to utilize the VA and the benefits they have earned and ensuring they recognize the valuable resources available to them.

Additionally, I organize workplace seminars where I share my mental-health journey with corporate audiences, underscoring the importance of support and the services provided through their employee benefits.

Yet, despite these professional and personal triumphs, I have grappled with the profound heartache that accompanies losing a loved one to suicide. Each year, I have mourned the passing of two to three friends from diverse backgrounds, including veterans and accomplished civilian professionals across various fields, to suicide. Some served alongside me in Iraq, while others epitomized the American dream. Behind their successes, however, many battled invisible struggles, suffering in silence without the necessary support—a harsh reality that has left a lasting impact on me. I wrote this book with these people in mind and to let you know that no matter how successful you are or where you are in life, it is okay to seek help. You are not alone; do not suffer in silence.

FROM DARKNESS TO HOPE

My experiences have not only shaped my career trajectory but have also deepened my commitment to mental-health advocacy. I emphasize the critical importance of support and awareness for those facing similar battles. Through this lens, I strive to grow both personally and professionally, fostering a culture of compassion and understanding within my circles.

The day I hit rock bottom, March 22, 2023, will forever be etched in my memory. I received devastating news: A friend I served with—a noncommissioned officer in my unit during our deployment in Iraq—had tragically committed murder-suicide. As the executive officer of Charlie Troop, 1st Cavalry, this individual, who was my mechanic, and I spent countless hours together ensuring that the troop's vehicles and weapons were fit for combat. The shocking nature of this event left me reeling, struggling to comprehend the actions of someone I had been close with—someone who had seemed committed to recovery and focused on his physical health and overall well-being.

The news shattered me. I was enveloped in profound sadness as I sat at my office desk, grappling with the harsh reality of the situation. In that moment, I felt an immense sense of loss for the victims and deep disbelief regarding how my friend could have descended into such darkness.

Compelled to share this heart-wrenching news with my boss and colleagues, I was overwhelmed by emotions that became unbearable. As I relayed the tragic information, I burst into uncontrollable weeping, the weight of grief crashing over me. At that moment, I questioned my own existence, and my mind went to a very dark place. As a father, thoughts of my child growing up without me overwhelmed me. I knew I wanted to be there to guide her through life for as long as possible, but at the same time,

I wanted my pain to disappear. In a state of shock and despair, I somehow made my way to the Charlotte Veterans Affairs Hospital. Upon my arrival, a compassionate therapist was assigned to help me process the traumatic news and navigate the overwhelming feelings that consumed me.

Honestly, it wasn't until I hit rock bottom—when the weight of my struggles became impossibly heavy—that I finally allowed medical professionals to step in and address my mental health officially. Up until that turning point, I had stubbornly resisted the idea of being diagnosed with PTSD or any other mental-health disorders. I had assumed I had PTSD simply as part of a conversation. However, after tests were conducted by medical professionals, I was assessed to have severe PTSD and other mental-health issues resulting from all the trauma and stress I had lived through. This assessment led to recommendations for counseling sessions and prescribed medication.

The idea of participating in weekly counseling sessions or taking prescribed medication felt like a betrayal to my self-image. It took me until the age of forty-five to muster the courage to face my reflection in the mirror. Now, I was not only prepared to acknowledge that I desperately needed help; I was in a position to actually receive the help I desperately needed.

The fear of seeking help loomed large for many reasons. Embarrassment was a significant barrier, intertwined with deep-rooted denial. After all, I had always been the dependable one at work and in my family, excelling in my finance career with an obsessive-compulsive attention to detail that garnered respect and admiration.

Ironically, the very traits that propelled me professionally began to strangle my personal relationships, suffocating any chance of genuine connection. I was paralyzed by the worry that others might label me as the "crazy army guy" or, worse, discover the medication in my medicine cabinet and redefine their perception of who I was at my core.

Even the idea of sitting down to discuss my demons brought waves of discomfort. The thought of committing to regular counseling had once overwhelmed me, but now I look forward to it. I feared the repercussions of taking time off work for therapy sessions, dreading the possibility of falling behind and losing the respect of my colleagues. After all, I was a combat arms veteran, inculcated with the belief that toughness was my defining attribute. I kept repeating to myself that nothing was wrong, clinging to the illusion that I could power through the pain alone.

RETHINKING MENTAL HEALTH IN THE WORKPLACE

In 2022, I was compelled to rethink my ideas on seeking help as I committed to a partner and welcomed a child into the world. This motivated me to live not just for myself but for my daughter's future, including her education and milestones, such as walking her down the aisle someday.

I recognized that no one is immune to mental-health struggles—regardless of wealth or intelligence—and I realized that sharing my story could assist others facing similar challenges.

Mental health affects families universally, often in ways that go unrecognized. It is vital that we take this issue seriously by exploring root causes and seeking ways to support employees who spend a significant portion of their lives at work. I aspire to be an advocate for mental-health awareness, understanding that while the disease may be invisible, effective counseling and proper medication can provide help. Open and honest communication with friends and family is crucial, as bottling up feelings or trying to escape through substances will ultimately lead to more problems.

It is important to recognize the significant impact of workplace culture on mental health. An inclusive environment promotes better collaboration, creativity, and support among team members. For example, my time in Wichita highlights that a lack of diverse perspectives can stifle innovation, teamwork, and overall momentum, leaving individuals feeling disconnected—especially someone like me, who thrives on interactions and may be suffering in silence.

Moreover, organizations must prioritize not only mental-health resources but also initiatives that promote work–life balance. Flexible working arrangements, regular check-ins, and open communication can significantly alleviate stress and encourage employees to prioritize their well-being.

From my own experience, I can attest that creating an environment where mental health is openly discussed and supported can empower individuals to seek help without fear of stigma.

It is essential to provide continuous education about mental health through resources such as workshops and access to counseling and to actively promote these resources to employees. This approach helps employees recognize and manage their mental-health challenges proactively. Looking back, I wish I had sought out these resources earlier in my career. Understanding the importance of mental wellness could have significantly detoured my path in a healthier direction. At that time, even the military did not encourage soldiers to seek mental-health treatment.

Ultimately, fostering a culture that recognizes the importance of mental health and actively supports it is a responsibility shared by employers and employees. By taking steps together, we can create healthier, more productive workplaces where everyone has the opportunity to thrive.

A JOURNEY TO MENTAL WELLNESS

At the New York Stock Exchange after ringing the bell

Daddy does hair

A happy family at the end of my mental wellness journey

As I reflect on the intricate tapestry of my life, I see a rich weave of triumphs, adversities, and profound growth. From my roots in the warm embrace of South Carolina to the disciplined halls of military training and finally the relentless currents of the corporate landscape, one undeniable truth stands out: The challenges of mental health are universal. They do not spare anyone based on age, occupation, or background. Trauma, in its myriad forms, can touch anyone—children, students, soldiers, professionals, and even those who seem to have it all. My narrative serves as a vivid testament to how resilience can be nurtured through life's trials, illustrating that seeking help is not a sign of weakness but rather a monumental act of strength.

Growing up in the South, I quickly learned that life is an unpredictable journey, often fraught with challenges. The early rupture of my parents' marriage left me grappling with deep-seated feelings of abandonment and insecurity. The transition to South Carolina, with its unfamiliar landscapes and faces, taught me vital lessons in adaptability while simultaneously sowing seeds of anxiety that would shadow my adulthood. Though my childhood was punctuated with moments of joy and connection, it was also marked by struggles that profoundly shaped my understanding of resilience. Little did I know then that those formative experiences were laying the groundwork for the formidable challenges that lay ahead.

My time as a soldier was nothing short of transformative. The rigorous training at West Point instilled within me a sense of discipline and purpose; however, it also exposed me to the brutal realities of mental strain. The relentless pace, immense pressure to excel, and unwavering need to prove my worth left deep scars that I carried into the tumultuous theaters of war in Kosovo and Iraq. Witnessing the complexities of combat—the sacrifices, heart-wrenching losses, and shared humanity with those on both sides—etched an indelible mark on my psyche. The camaraderie with my fellow soldiers offered profound strength, yet the staggering weight of responsibility and the haunting traumas of battle often felt like burdens too heavy to bear.

As I transitioned into the corporate world, I held on to the hope that those struggles were a thing of the past. Yet, I quickly realized they had followed me into this new arena. The high-octane environment of investment banking combined with the lingering shadows of PTSD concocted a perfect storm. I found myself ensnared in battles against anxiety, insomnia, and feelings of profound isolation. In spite of my professional achievements, I often felt like I was just barely keeping my head above water. It wasn't until I hit the depths of despair that I finally acknowledged the necessity of asking for help. Seeking counseling and embracing the support of others transformed my trajectory.

Through every twist and turn, I've learned that mental-health struggles are not exclusive to soldiers or those scarred by combat. Trauma can arise from a vast array of sources: childhood experiences, academic pressures, career stress, or personal losses. It can touch anyone regardless of accomplishments or outward facades. The stigma surrounding mental health can create barriers that prevent individuals from seeking the help they desperately need, but I've discovered there's no shame in leaning on others. In fact, it is one of the bravest steps a person can take.

Resilience is not merely about facing life's challenges in solitude; it's about finding the courage to lean on others when you need it most. Whether it's a trusted friend, a family member, or a compassionate professional, the support from those around you can become a vital lifeline. My journey proves that vulnerability is not an indication of weakness—it's a pathway to healing and transformation. By sharing my story, I hope to encourage others to embrace their unique journeys, seek help when necessary, and recognize that they are never truly alone.

As I look toward the horizon, I am resolutely committed to advocating for mental-health awareness and fostering a culture of compassion and understanding. Whether in our workplaces, military institutions, or personal lives, we all have an essential role in supporting one another. Life is a journey filled with peaks and valleys, but with resilience, hope, and the openness to seek help, we can navigate its myriad challenges and emerge from them stronger than before.

To anyone reading this, I want you to know it's not only okay to ask for help, it's a courageous act to reach out and lean on others. It's perfectly valid to take the time you need to heal. Your journey is uniquely yours, and your resilience stands as a powerful testament to your strength. Together, we can cultivate a world where mental health is prioritized and every individual has the opportunity to thrive.

CONTACT ME

I would love to engage your organization in discussions about my mental-health journey. Sharing experiences can greatly benefit both employees and employers. If your firm aims to foster a supportive environment, please reach out via email at omarritter@gmail.com. You can also visit my LinkedIn profile at www.linkedin.com/in/omar-ritter-cpa-sphr/ or my website at www.omarritter.com/ for more insights.

In addition to motivational speaking, I serve as an area president and fractional CFO at FocusCFO, where we help business owners gain financial control to support their goals. Many of our team members hold the Certified Exit Planner (CEPA) designation. To learn more about our services, visit www.focuscfo.com or contact me at o.ritter@focuscfo.com.

ADDITIONAL RESOURCES

You can find valuable resources in the chart below to further assist in promoting mental well-being in your organization.

NAME OF THE ORGANIZATION	DESCRIPTION	SERVICES PROVIDED	CONTACT INFORMATION
National Suicide Prevention Lifeline	Provides 24/7, free and confidential support for people in distress, prevention and crisis resources for individuals and families	Crisis intervention, emotional support, and referrals to local resources	Website: suicidepreventionlifeline.org Email: info@suicidepreventionlifeline.org Phone: 1-800-273-8255
Crisis Text Line	Offers free, 24/7 support for those in crisis via text messaging	Crisis intervention and emotional support through text messaging	Website: crisistextline.org Email: support@crisistextline.org Phone: Text "HELLO" to 741741

NAME OF THE ORGANIZATION	DESCRIPTION	SERVICES PROVIDED	CONTACT INFORMATION
NAMI Helpline	Provides information and support for people affected by mental health conditions and families	Education, advocacy, and support services for individuals and families	Website: nami.org Email: info@nami.org Phone: 1-800-950-NAMI (6264)
Anxiety and Depression Association of America (ADAA)	Offers resources, support, and treatment information for individuals with anxiety and depression	Education, online resources, support groups, and referrals to mental health professionals	Website: adaa.org Email: information@adaa.org Phone: 240-485-1001
PTSD Foundation of America	Provides support and resources for veterans and individuals affected by post-traumatic stress disorder (PTSD)	Peer support, counseling, education, and outreach programs	Website: ptsdusa.org Email: info@ptsdusa.org Phone: 877-717-PTSD (7873)
Mental Health America (MHA)	Promotes awareness and resources for individuals living with mental health conditions	Education, screening tools, support groups, and advocacy services	Website: mhanational.org Email: info@mhanational.org Phone: 1-800-273-TALK (8255)

ABOUT THE AUTHOR

OMAR RITTER is a dynamic storyteller and accomplished author renowned for his ability to deftly examine the themes of resilience, personal growth, and overcoming adversity. With a rich life woven of diverse experiences, Omar's journey began in humble surroundings and has taken him from delivering newspapers as a boy to facing the challenges of West Point and serving in combat to ultimately achieving success in the cutthroat world of Wall Street.

Omar holds a Bronze Star and Combat Action Badge for his exemplary leadership during operations in Iraq. Since leaving the military, he has enjoyed a distinguished career as a finance and accounting executive. Omar's academic achievements, which include an MBA from Columbia Business School and a bachelor's degree in mechanical engineering from West Point, provided the tools he used to excel as a Certified Public Accountant, Chartered Global Management Accountant, Certified Exit Planning Advisor, and Senior Professional in Human Resources.

Having spent over twenty years grappling with post-traumatic stress disorder (PTSD) and various other mental-health challenges, Omar's firsthand experiences fuel his passion for breaking the stigma surrounding such issues. He aspires to help others navigate their own struggles by sharing his story and advocating for mental wellness. Now residing in Charlotte, North Carolina, with his wife and daughter, Omar's writing is infused with wisdom and compassion, encouraging readers to embrace their own journeys toward healing and resilience.

Through his engaging narratives, Omar not only captivates his audience but also empowers them to confront their inner battles with courage and hope. His unwavering positivity and insightful reflections resonate deeply with his readers, inspiring a transformative perspective on life's challenges and the strength found in vulnerability.

www.ingramcontent.com/pod-product-compliance
Lightning Source LLC
Chambersburg PA
CBHW060521080526
44586CB00012B/569